The
Library of

SCIENCE AND SOCIETY
1600–1900

SCIENCE AND SOCIETY
1600–1900

by

P. M. RATTANSI   D. S. L. CARDWELL
A. RUPERT HALL   E. M. SIGSWORTH
PETER MATHIAS   ROY M. MACLEOD

Edited by

PETER MATHIAS

Chichele Professor of Economic History,
University of Oxford

CAMBRIDGE

At the University Press

1972

Published by the Syndics of the Cambridge University Press
Bentley House, 200 Euston Road, London NW1 2DB
American Branch: 32 East 57th Street, New York, N.Y.10022

Library of Congress Catalogue Card Number: 76-172833

ISBN: 0 521 08375 3

Printed in Great Britain by
Alden & Mowbray Ltd
at the Alden Press, Oxford

CONTENTS

List of Plates   *page* vi
Preface   vii

1   The social interpretation of science in the seven-
    teenth century
        by P. M. Rattansi   1

2   Science, technology and Utopia in the seventeenth
    century
        by A. Rupert Hall   33

3   Who unbound Prometheus? Science and technical
    change, 1600–1800
        by Peter Mathias   54

4   Science and the steam engine, 1790–1825
        by D. S. L. Cardwell   81

5   Gateways to death? Medicine, hospitals and mor-
    tality, 1700–1850
        by E. M. Sigsworth   97

6   Resources of science in Victorian England: the
    Endowment of Science Movement, 1868–1900
        by Roy M. MacLeod   111

PLATES

Between pages 96 and 97

1A   A German double-acting column-of-water engine fitted with Watt's parallel motion

1B   Richard Trevithick's double-acting column-of-water engine as installed at the Wheal Druid mine, Cornwall

2   Strutt's Mill at Belper

3   Diagram of a double-acting column-of-water engine

4   Column-of-water engine at a mine in Schemnitz (Banska Stiavnica, Slovakia)

Facing page 136

5   Men in possession

PREFACE

This collection of essays had its origin in a series of public lectures which I was asked to arrange by the History and Philosophy of Science Committee at Cambridge – the interfaculty body which bears responsibility for determining the academic programme in this subject. The lectures were delivered during the Michaelmas Term 1968. As a 'lay' member of the committee, representing the History Faculty, it was thought appropriate that the theme for the lectures should be 'science and society'; a series of explorations of major issues where science had interacted with economic, social and intellectual sequences in the development of Western society. Thus, historians who are concerned with the evolution of science primarily from a range of interests and relationships beyond that of science itself are contributors to this volume with historians of science themselves. This reflects a significant increase in interest in the history of science from a diversity of historical viewpoints – here mainly by economic historians interested in different links between science and technical change in economic development, but this is one facet of a much wider and more diversified concern. Science as an intellectual and practical activity has impacted upon so many different aspects of human development – intellectual and philosophical, economic and social, cultural, demographic, etc. – that these 'external' relationships and interactions form a crucially important area of research for the history of science itself. The new commitment of the Wellcome Foundation in the 'social history of medicine' is a recognition of this trend.

Most studies in the history of science, particularly 'subject' studies covering the development of individual sciences, have been 'internal' in their scope and objectives, plotting progress within the different branches of science as the frontiers of knowledge about formal scientific relationships get pushed back by intellectual advance. The history of science is thus seen primarily as a record of progressive intellectual discovery at the hands of individual genius. The 'external' relations of science, investigations into the impact of scientific knowledge within its wider historical context (and the impact of that context, both material and intellectual, upon the development of science) has received much less attention. It is a field where co-operation between historians of science and other historians will yield great benefits to both parties, even if, as is likely, conflicts of interpretation prove to be very much greater than with the 'internal' history of science. Such conflicts will yield much greater intellectual sophistication to their participants – to historians of science whose technical expertise has sometimes flourished at the expense of a more general historical naïveté and to other historians whose theorising has often been much facilitated by their ignorance of scientific and technological knowledge.

The 'internal' history of science, in its simpler manifestations, has also tended to emphasise the logical coherence of intellectual structure and the steady accretion of knowledge (if not a progressive revelation towards a latter-day absolute truth) over time. Such Whiggish, historicist tendencies in the historiography of science will be made more difficult to sustain as the growth of science is analysed within its historical context, philosophical no less than material. But in history, a disappointingly inexact discipline if intellectual activities be judged according to their amenability to general statements, truth is often bought at the cost of methodological simplicity.

PETER MATHIAS

All Souls College, Oxford
January 1972

1

THE SOCIAL INTERPRETATION
OF SCIENCE IN THE
SEVENTEENTH CENTURY

by P. M. Rattansi

I

The 1930s were the heyday of the social interpretation of seventeenth-century science. The great development of modern physical science in the sixteenth and seventeenth centuries was related to contemporary social and economic changes by Marxist and neo-Marxist authors. Boris Hessen attributed the creation of the new science to the economic needs of the rising *bourgeoisie* and connected the most abstract propositions of Newton's *Principia* with the technical needs of the mercantile class of seventeenth-century England.[1] Edger Zilsel suggested that a dramatic lowering of the class barriers which had prevented any dialogue between the scholar and the craftsman since the ancients, resulted in a fusion of empiricism and rationalism and the birth of a new kind of science in post-Renaissance Italy.[2]

A more cautious approach was represented by the American sociologist Robert K. Merton.[3] Developing an insight buried in Max Weber's famous investigation of the relation between Calvinist Puritanism and capitalism, Merton came to the conclusion that Puritan values had been important in seventeenth-century England in concentrating a great deal of attention upon the study of the natural sciences. At the same time, he investigated the influence of economic and technological motives in the selective attention given to the physical

[1] 'The Social and Economic Roots of Newton's "Principia" ', in *Science at the Cross Roads*, n.d. (1932).

[2] 'The Sociological Roots of Science', *American Journal of Sociology*, XLVII (1942).

[3] 'Science, Technology and Society in Seventeenth Century England', *Osiris*, IV (1938), 414–565.

sciences, and to particular topics within these sciences, and concluded that it was far from negligible.

Neither historians nor sociologists have shown much interest in the social interpretation of seventeenth-century science for some decades. There was a strong reaction against crudely Marxist interpretations, and against the sociology of knowledge itself. The brilliant explorations of the intellectual structure of the new science which were pioneered by E. A. Burtt, Ernst Cassirer, and Alexandre Koyré have absorbed their attention for nearly a generation. There are signs of a revival of interest in the social setting of early modern science, partly a by-product of the renewed attention to the relation between science and society. It may be valuable to re-examine Merton's thesis in the light of recent historical research, in order to clarify our thoughts about problems and approaches in that area of historical studies.

II

Merton's thesis has not lacked critics in recent years. Some of them entirely dismiss the possibility of a sociology of science. The history of science, they argue, is essentially like the history of philosophy. To study its social and economic setting contributes nothing to its understanding as a structure of ideas. In its extreme form, that attitude has probably ceased to command general assent among historians of science. If science is to be studied as a system of ideas, then its insulation from other sorts of ideas and (since at least some of these may be more sensitive to influences originating in the sociological context) from society has to be investigated for each period and problem, and cannot be assumed in advance. All the more is it true of the 'new science' which had to develop outside the traditional framework of higher education and, indeed, to oppose the natural philosophy taught at the universities. It had to compete with the more conventional pursuits in attracting the interest and patronage of the cultivated amateur. The ruling Aristotelian natural philosophy was intimately associated with a Christian-scholastic theological world-picture, and any rival system had perforce to define its consonance, or even more, its superiority as the basis for a genuinely Christian world-picture. With few exceptions, the major natural philosophers of the period fully recognised the intimate connection between their scientific work and their philosophical, social, ethical, and, above all, religious concerns. The sensitivity of the natural sciences to sociological influence in their claim to be a focus of intellectual interest is all too plain today, when the 'flight from science' is exercising the most technically advanced and industrialised countries of the world. This applies even when the natural sciences are legitimated and institutionalised within the system of higher education and integrated within the professional structure. That should make it superfluous to argue the point at very great length today.

Merton was, therefore, raising an important question when he asked why the study of nature should have succeeded in attracting such a major share of attention in seventeenth-century England, when it had no secure foothold in the contemporary educational or occupational structure, and was not capable of commending itself by solving outstanding technological problems. That there was a shift of interest towards science, at the expense of other pursuits, he established by an interesting statistical survey of the seventeenth-century Englishmen listed in the *Dictionary of National Biography*.

The influence of religion in either attracting men towards or away from scientific studies appeared an important subject for inquiry in a predominantly religious period. R. F. Jones and Dorothy Stimson had already regarded Puritanism as a favourable influence. Merton greatly elaborated these views, and suggested that Puritanism, as a structure of values which had moulded English thought in general during this period in fundamental ways, had created not only a consonance between its religious ethic and experimental science, but provided a powerful religious motive for actively engaging in its pursuit. Those values encouraged a commitment to the study of God's 'Book of Nature' as complementing the study of the book of God's word. They imposed a religious obligation to make such study serve the twin ends of glorifying God and benefiting fellow-men. They supported a combined empirical and rational method as the instrument of scientific knowledge. The Calvinist doctrine of predestination had saddled men with the tormenting problem of gaining some insight into their own

3

eternal destiny. Although good works could not purchase grace, they became a sign of it, and scientific studies came to be prominently included amongst them. Merton believed that his study of the founders of the Royal Society and of its membership during the post-Restoration period, confirmed the hypothesis that Puritan values had played an important role in directing men to the study of nature.

Much of the criticism of Merton's thesis in recent years has concentrated on his definition of Puritan values. A far more general charge, however, could be made about that pioneer study today: its surprising lack of feeling for the texture of social, political, and religious history of seventeenth-century England, or of contemporary scientific thought. If Puritanism was of crucial importance in raising science to a prominent intellectual position, then the mid-century period of Puritan dominance should have occupied an important place in Merton's investigation. Nineteenth-century historians of education had already noticed the numerous projects for the introduction of scientific teaching among the many proposals made during the revolutionary period. Yet Merton chose to dismiss this period with some remarks on the discouragement that scientific studies must suffer during a troubled time, although his enumeration of 'Puritan scientists' included prominent reformers of that period like Samuel Hartlib and John Dury, John Webster and Noah Biggs.

Nor did Merton choose to discriminate between the very different sorts of conceptions of 'new science' which competed for dominance after the discrediting of Aristotelian-scholastic philosophy, or discuss the mechanical world-view whose triumph by the mid-seventeenth century was of such enormous significance. The neglect would presumably be justified on the ground that the sociologist is concerned with the extent to which the study of nature served as a dominant interest, whatever the theories held about it. Nevertheless, it is conceivable that different sorts of ideals of the nature of the scientific enterprise may have appealed to different sorts of motives, including the religious motives to which Merton gave so much attention. The lack of interest in the detailed history of scientific ideas has naturally led to charges that Merton thought of science as a bag of tricks for technological control over nature, while overlooking its profound intellectual challenge, and that such cross head-counting cannot enhance our understanding of the science of the period.

An important modification of Merton's thesis is suggested when closer attention is given to the various sorts of 'new science' which competed as successors to the Aristotelianism of the schools, and especially to a current which has been explored in greater detail in recent years: Renaissance Hermeticism. Most of the motives which Merton regarded as providing a consonance between Puritanism and science are, indeed, to be found intertwined in the development of Hermeticism in the Protestant lands from the late sixteenth century onwards.

The links between Hermeticism and 'new science', and between Puritanism, science, and the 'Puritan Revolution' can be discussed together. Many of the prominent examples cited by Merton to support the connection between Puritanism and science, men like Hartlib, Dury, Comenius, John Webster, and Noah Biggs, belonged essentially to that tradition.

III

In his great study of the development of the Hermetic writings in late antiquity, Father Festugière has traced the progressive undermining of the Aristotelian ideal of disinterested knowledge in the Hellenistic world, especially in Egypt.[1] An ideal which valued understanding above practical application gave way to one of knowledge for immediate personal gain, whether by attaining knowledge of the future (astrology), or creating fabulous wealth (alchemy), or conferring mastery over nature and ensuring salvation in the after-life (magic and the occult sciences). Unlike Aristotelianism, which subordinated the particular to the general, the individual to the universal, the new approach focussed attention on properties specific to each particular thing, preferably on extraordinary and marvellous virtues, or *mirabilia*. The aim was to grasp the hidden powers of nature and the mysterious forces typified by attraction and repulsion: what the collectors of *mirabilia*,

---

[1] A.-J. Festugière, *La Révélation d'Hermès Trismegiste*, Paris (1950–4), 4 vols. also 'L'Hermetisme', *Bull. Soc. Roy. des Lettres de Lund*, I (1947–8), 1–58.

especially Pliny, called the laws of sympathy and antipathy between things. Such modes of action were supposed to characterise all the three kingdoms of nature. Under the influence of astrological doctrines, the stars were thought to govern the mysterious sympathies and antipathies between things. In the course of time, a hierarchy of beings came to be suspended from a particular star, from angels down to minerals, deriving their virtues from the star. He who knew these secrets would know how to obtain the desired result by cutting a certain plant, or attempting the transmutation of a particular metal, or ingesting a certain drug, at a particular time.

Such a view promoted a sharp break with the Aristotelian assumption of the capacity of human reason to penetrate to first principles. If knowledge of nature was primarily the knowledge of occult virtues and secret sympathies and antipathies, it could come only from a revelation, from a blinding vision vouchsafed by a divinity.

In the Mediterranean countries and the trans-Alpine lands in which Hermetic ideas were to be assimilated and developed in the late fifteenth and sixteenth centuries, various forces combined to undermine scholastic Aristotelianism as the dominant philosophy. The attempt to combine Aristotelian naturalism with Christian dogma created tensions which even the magnificent Thomistic synthesis could not suppress. In the fourteenth and fifteenth centuries the nominalist critique of the possibilities of a rational theology gained importance at many universities. Moreover, the growth of the secular sphere of life and the legitimation of its concerns, combined with the breaking of the clerical monopoly of intellectual roles, promoted a practical orientation unfavourable to the contemplative rationalism enshrined in Aristotelianism. Aristotelian doctrine, encyclopaedic and coherent at the same time, embodying a vision of intellectual unity that has never again been recaptured, steered a subtle middle way between the religious-mystical sensibility of Plato and the materialism of the earlier natural philosophers. When suitably modified, it had served as the world-view of three theocentric cultures at a certain stage of their development: of Islam, Judaism, and Christianity, cultures in which the intellectual and religious roles were essentially fused. As life-conditions in the

Italian city-states became closer to those of the classical world, so the cultivated upper-classes and intellectuals found their cultural ideal in one major culture in which Aristotelian teaching had never become an orthodoxy – the Republican Rome of the time of Cicero. Educational preparation came to be far more highly valued, but the emphasis shifted towards the *studia humanitatis* of grammar, rhetoric, history, poetry, and moral philosophy, which appeared far more relevant to life in the city-state than dialectic, logic, natural philosophy, and the professional disciplines. The feeling that Aristotelianism and its subtle categories did not provide an appropriate conceptual structure for their thought and experience led humanists to adopt an eclectic attitude to philosophy of the sort typified by the admired Cicero. Meanwhile, in the North, Aristotelianism was undercut by various lay movements counselling an emotional religiosity instead of a learned and excessively intellectual approach to faith, and merging into the initial anti-intellectualism of the Reformation period.

By the sixteenth century north-western Europe, too, was swept into an era of swift and bewildering change, disrupting tradition and traditional relationships through the pressure of new economic, social, religious, and intellectual forces. The resulting crisis in intellectual life has left a great monument in Montaigne's *Apologie de Raimond Sebond* (1580). Montaigne depicted the questioning of the inherited picture of the world as the Reformation shattered the unity of Christendom, and religious conflicts, especially the Wars of Religion in France, destroyed the illusion of the perfection of Christian societies. At the same time, the geographical discoveries forced a revaluation of the idea of Europe as a model Christian society. Mental horizons were extended in another dimension by the humanists who recovered a whole world of classical thought which, however, was now seen to exhibit far greater conflict and diversity than had been evident from the few ancients who dominated scholastic teaching. The authority of the ancients themselves had been challenged by such men as Copernicus and Paracelsus.

In sum, the individual was confronted with an enormously wider range of competing beliefs in almost every area of social and intellectual concern, while conformity-inducing pressures of a mainly ecclesiastical sort were weakened or discredited. Of the various responses to this situation, two are of particular interest for us. There was, first, a re-structuring of scholastic Aristotelianism to meet the new challenges. Luther was critical of the 'heathen' Aristotle in his early reforming zeal, but with the triumph of the Reformation did not dissent from his associate Melanchthon's conviction that there was no viable alternative to Aristotelian teaching as the basis of the intellectual culture imparted at the Protestant universities.[1] Protestant neo-scholasticism borrowed a great deal from the revitalisation of Aristotelian teaching by the learned Jesuit commentators of the Iberian peninsula.[2] At some of the Italian universities, notably at Padua, a 'purified' Aristotelianism provided the background for important advances in the life sciences.[3]

The second type of response was a recourse to magical techniques in the sophisticated philosophical version of the Hermetics and neo-Platonists of late antiquity, to relieve anxiety and confer at least the illusion of control when traditional modes of dealing with the world seemed to be breaking down. It must not be forgotten, however, that in their Renaissance interpretation, these doctrines helped to rehabilitate a new vision of the importance and dignity of man in the universe.

Historians of the culture of the Renaissance have paid much attention to the influence of neo-Platonic doctrines on the art and culture of the Renaissance. Throughout the sixteenth century they were enormously important in northern Europe, in the form given to them by the Florentine thinkers Marsilio Ficino and Pico della Mirandola, in reconciling the lay emotional piety of the trans-Alpine lands with the humanistic ideals of the Italian Renaissance. Neo-Platonic ideas enhanced both the self-image and the public image of architecture, painting, and sculpture at a time when their practitioners were trying to raise themselves from their medieval assimilation to the crafts. In artistic creation, man imitated the divine and

1 Heinrich Boehmer, *Martin Luther: Road to Reformation*, Eng. tr. (London, 1957), pp. 28, 159.
2 P. Peterson, *Geschichte der aristotelischen Philosophie im protestantischen Deutschland* (Leipzig, 1921).
3 Walter Pagel, *William Harvey's Biological Ideas* (Basel & New York, 1967).

came closest to God. Through the beauty and harmony of the work of art, the artist carried the mind of the spectator to the suprasensual realm of divine archetypes. Such ideas were not confined to the plastic arts, but influenced technologists and those devising new mechanical inventions. They, too, invoked the analogy with the divine work of constructing the 'machine of the world' to lend greater prestige to their own work. They justified hopes of great marvels being accessible through their work by citing a celebrated section of the *Corpus Hermeticum* which described how the ancient Egyptians made statues that moved and spoke by drawing down the Spirit of the World into them.[1] Cornelius Agrippa spoke in 1526 of 'many other imitators of nature, wise inquirers into hidden things who ... confidently undertake, only by mathematical learning and the help of celestial influences to produce many miraculous works, such as walking and speaking bodies ... '[2] John Wilkins, writing in 1648, referred to the attempts of some Paracelsians to attain perpetual motion by relying upon the microcosm-macrocosm analogy and the power of the *anima mundi*.[3]

These ambitions only made sense within a magical view of nature, which saw a difference only of degree between the *power* of an artistic representation, and that ascribed to amulets, gems inscribed with planetary symbols, or Cabbalistic numbers; or between the mechanical marvels described in the recovered works of Hero of Alexandria, the legendary artificial dove of Archytas and planetarium of Archimedes, and the walking and speaking statues attributed to Hermes Trismegistus. Such a re-enchantment of the world was an integral part of the teaching of the Florentine Platonists. Pico's 'Oration on the Dignity of Man' saw that dignity as residing precisely in man as *magus*, who:

in calling forth into the light as if from their hiding-places the powers scattered and sown in the world by the loving-kindness of God, does not

---

[1] F. A. Yates, *Giordano Bruno and the Hermetic Tradition* (London, 1964), p. 37.

[2] *De incertitudine et vanitate scientiarum* (1531), cited from Eng. tr. (London, 1694), p. 112.

[3] *Mathematical Magick*, cited from *The Mathematical and Philosophical Works of the Right Rev. John Wilkins* (London, 1802), vol. II, pp. 212–14; compare J. J. Becher's machine described by Oldenburg to Hartlib in 1658 in A. R. & M. B. Hall, eds., *The Correspondence of Henry Oldenburg* (Madison & Milwaukee, 1965), vol. II, pp. 186–7.

so much work wonders as diligently serve a wonder-working nature ...
having more searchingly examined into the harmony of the universe ...
and having clearly perceived the reciprocal affinity of natures, and
applying to each single thing the suitable and peculiar inducements ...
brings forth into the open the miracles concealed in the recesses of the
world, in the depths of nature, and in the storehouses and mysteries of
God, just as if she herself were their maker; and, as the farmer weds his
elms to vines, even so does the *magus* wed earth to heaven, that is, he
weds lower things to the endowments and powers of higher things ... (it)
rouses him (man) to the admiration of God's works, which is the most
certain condition of a willing faith, hope, and love ...[1]

The magic of Ficino and Pico, of Reuchlin and Cornelius
Agrippa was a revival of late-antique and cabbalistic doctrines.
The *magus* would work wonders through his knowledge of the
secret laws of sympathy and antipathy in the universe and of
the vivifying and restorative powers of the stars. Such powers
would be used to benefit the individual or his friends, for
example, in relieving the scholarly disease of 'melancholy'.[2]
There was little place in this conception for the idea of novelty
or discovery. The aim was the restoration of a body of esoteric
knowledge, hidden in ancient myth and fable, in the *Corpus
Hermeticum*, and in the numerical symbolism of the Cabbala.

It was in the work of Paracelsus (1494–1541) that the neo-
Platonic and Hermetic heritage was transformed until it
came to be considered a serious rival to the scholastic-Aris-
totelian natural philosophy well into the seventeenth century.
Underlying the complex and labyrinthine doctrines of Paracelsus was a consistent fidelity to the neo-Platonic vision of a
visible world which was merely the outward covering of an
invisible world of active power continually infused into all
things from the fount of all power. That justified the rejection
of the element-theories of the ancients, and dissolved the
notion of matter into that of patterns of spiritual powers.
Man was, indeed, a microcosm. He contained the constituents
of all things in heaven and earth. The universe could be studied
by studying man like a book; on the other hand, man could
be understood by a study of the macrocosm of the universe

1 Published 1487. Cited from tr. by E. L. Forbes in E. Cassirer *et al. The Renaissance
Philosophy of Man* (Chicago, 1958), pp. 248–9.
2 R. Klibansky, E. Panofsky & F. Saxl, *Saturn and Melancholy* (London, 1964);
D. P. Walker, *Spiritual & Demonic Magic from Ficino to Campanella* (London,
1958).

and the geocosm of the earth. Since man united all things in himself, he could achieve that knowledge at a far deeper level than that of discursive reason, through an act of sympathetic attraction between an object and its inner representative in man's own constitution.[1]

The interest in the particular and the specific, rather than the general and universal, which Festugière regards as an essential characteristic of late-antique magic, was the *leitmotiv* of Paracelsian doctrine. The almost infinite diversity manifested in the universe made any attempt to bring it under a few general principles, derived by reason and logic, false and sinful. Like his anti-Lutheran 'Spiritualist' associates, who stressed inward experience against Biblical fundamentalism, Paracelsus emphasised the union with the object through 'experience' above all written texts, however ancient and hallowed. Experiment could mean the chance observation of the therapeutic properties of a plant; through 'experience', which 'overheard' the *scientia* or principle of operation of the plant, it would be converted into the surest kind of knowledge.[2] Paracelsus' procedure may seem particularly well adapted to a programme for discovering the therapeutic virtues of various substances and extending the *pharmacopaiea* inherited from the Greeks and Arabic physicians and traditionally understood in terms of the Aristotelian theory of elements and complexions. He himself aspired to nothing less than a universal science of nature.[3]

Paracelsus believed that God aimed at two things in His creation: that nothing remained hidden but all became visible and revealed, and that whatever He had made but left incomplete should be brought to completion. Man fulfilled both purposes, by knowing things, and by acting as an 'alchemist', that is, one who brought things to their perfection. It was a continuing process, and new things could be discovered that were unknown to the ancients and the Arabs.[4] In some of his writings, Paracelsus subscribed to the eschatological

---

[1] W. Pagel, *Paracelsus, An Introduction to Philosophical Medicine in the Era of the Renaissance* (Basel & New York, 1958), pp. 54–64.

[2] *Ibid.* p. 60.

[3] A. G. Debus, *The Chemical Dream of the Renaissance* (Churchill College Lecture 3, Cambridge, 1968).

[4] J. Jacobi, ed. *Paracelsus, Selected Writings* (London, 1951), p. 203.

mood of his 'Spiritualist' friends, and foresaw the dawning oι the Joachimite age of the Holy Spirit in which nothing would remain hidden and arts and sciences would attain their greatest perfection.[1]

The conviction that the millennium was imminent inspired various thinkers in the Germanic lands in the late sixteenth and early seventeenth century. They were particularly attracted by Paracelsian doctrines. Besides converting the macrocosm–microcosm analogy into a tool for the investigation of nature and affirming the central importance of manual operations and experience in such investigation, Paracelsus differed from ancient and contemporary Hermeticism in dedicating the fruits of knowledge to the larger social-Christian ends of relieving misery and suffering. These ideas were congenial to the millennial utopianism of such men as Johannes Alsted (1588–1638), Johann Valentin Andreae (1586–1654), and J. A. Comenius (1592–1671). Their social, religious, and educational reform was based on the conviction that the millennium was at hand, and would be marked by the recovery of the knowledge of creatures that Adam had possessed in his innocence, and of the Adamic language which had given him power over all things.

The idea of studying nature to glorify God and benefit mankind through inventions and discoveries was therefore something of a commonplace by the time Francis Bacon (1561–1626) made it the dominant theme of his reformation of all learning. Bacon recognised that the alchemist and natural magician shared his aim to study nature 'with a view to works'.[2] The true and lawful goal of the sciences was that 'human life be endowed with discoveries and powers'.[3] Man had lost his dominion over creatures with the Fall. A new age was dawning when man would recover his powers. He must renounce the intellectual pride enshrined in the logical-dialectical method of Aristotle, and in the belief that 'the dignity of the human mind is impaired by long and close intercourse with experiments and particulars ... '[4] Not through

[1] *Ibid.* p. 296.
[2] *Works*, ed. Spedding, Ellis, & Heath (London, 1857–9), *Novum Organum* (Bk. I, Aph. v), vol. IV, pp. 47–8.
[3] *Ibid.* (Bk. I, Aph. lxxxi), IV, p. 79.
[4] *Ibid.* (Bk. I, Aph. lxxxiii), IV, p. 81; *Adv. Lear.* bk. 2, I, 5.

lazy observances, but only 'if we labour in thy works with the sweat of our brows, thou will make us partakers of thy vision and thy sabbath'.[1] Only the mechanical arts, which the learned man was apt to despise, were 'continually growing and becoming more perfect', while the sciences were more likely to show corruption and degeneration over time.[2]

But while endorsing their aims and their insistence on the experience gained through manual operations, Bacon found much to condemn in the Hermetics and natural magicians, especially in their corrupting philosophy by 'superstition and an admixture of theology'.[3] Bacon's scientific enterprise was dedicated to a supremely religious end, and he believed it constituted the truest form of religious worship. But it was to be conducted by a 'legitimate, chaste, and severe course of inquiry' which excluded the mixture of secular and religious knowledge, for 'from this unwholesome mixture of things human and divine there arises not only a fantastic philosophy but also a heretical religion'.[4] Bacon particularly castigated 'the school of Paracelsus, and some others, that have pretended to find the truth of all natural philosophy in the Scriptures ... '[5] He condemned the Paracelsian attempt to find 'in man's body certain correspondencies and parallels which have respect to all the several species (as stars, planets, minerals) which are extant in the universe ... '[6] The human senses and understanding were not to be 'deprived of their authority, but to be supplied with helps'.[7]

Bacon's transformation of the Hermetic dream can best be appreciated by recapitulating the essential characteristics of the latter. The neo-Platonic conception of God and His relation to the universe, as interpreted by the Florentine thinkers and others throughout the sixteenth century, stressed His will rather than His reason, and the ways in which that will was made manifest in the universe through His continually active and creative power. It restored a highly 'enchanted' conception of the universe, with man at the centre of a web of hidden correspondencies and sympathies and antipathies.

[1] *Ibid.* IV, p. 33.
[2] *Ibid.* (Bk. I, Aph. lxxiv), IV, pp. 74–5; preface to 'The Great Instauration'.
[3] *Ibid.* (Bk. I, Aph. lxv), IV, p. 65.
[4] *Ibid.* IV, p. 66.   [5] *Adv. Lear.*, in *ibid.*, III, pp. 485–6.
[6] *Ibid.* III, p. 370.   [7] *Nov. Org.* (Bk. I, Aph. lxvii) in *ibid.* p. 69.

Wedded to an active ideal of life, it suggested ways of capturing that power for human ends. Knowledge of the correspondencies lay beyond rational comprehension since not only genera and species but each particular object depended for its specific virtues and properties upon its archetype. That knowledge could be attained only through illumination, grace, the scripture, esoteric ancient texts like the Hermetics' writings, and (especially for Paracelsus) observation and manual experiments. Language, mathematical symbols, and works of art were all charged with power since they corresponded to the divine archetypes.

For the 'Northern Renaissance', Florentine Platonism permitted a legitimation of delight in the flesh and in the natural world through a highly-charged spiritualisation of the universe. It helped to adapt Christian belief to an increasingly secularised society by drawing upon classical Graeco–Roman ideals in the guise of borrowings from the Hebrews. The ambition of attaining powers to relieve disease and augment human labour, too, emerged within a religious framework. It made extensive use of such notions as those of a *spiritus*, neither matter nor soul, which traversed the universe and carried the power of higher beings to lower ones.[1] In actively labouring and creating, man came nearest to God who was above all an ever-generative God. In grasping the powers and virtues that God has infused and sustained in things, and in working with them, man re-attained the dignity with which he was clothed at the first Creation. The Reformation, too, aimed at recovering an intense spirituality in place of intellectual systems and the externals of faith. It gave Hermeticism a more strident anti-intellectualism and anti-authoritarianism, emphasised scripture as the source of valid knowledge, and harnessed it to larger Christian-utopian hopes.

The eschatological mood and the atmosphere of 'primitive Christianity' had nourished the Reformation. Its persistence became a major problem for the leaders of the Reformation as they consolidated their victory amidst the protests of those who saw their hopes of a new Jerusalem defeated by the bargains struck with worldly powers. No authority was secure

---

[1] F. Sherwood Taylor, 'The Idea of the Quintessence', in E. A. Underwood, ed. *Science, Medicine and History* (London, 1953), I, pp. 247–65.

as long as men were possessed by the conceit of enjoying (as Bacon's near-contemporary, Richard Hooker wrote in 1594/7) 'the special illumination of the Holy Ghost, whereby they discern those things in the Word, which others reading, yet discern them not'.[1] They were beyond argument:

Be they Women, or be they Men, if once they have tasted of that Cup, let any man of contrary opinion open his mouth to perswade them, they close up their ears, his Reasons they weigh not, all is answered with rehearsal of the words of *John, We are of God;* he that knoweth God heareth us. As for the rest, *Ye are of the World* . . .

Bacon reflected a widespread conviction that the restoration of stability and order was necessary no less in intellectual matters than in the social, political, and religious spheres where a century of swift change had brought about a series of crises. Authority had to be re-established in the arts and sciences by defining once again the relation between the recognised sources of valid knowledge. Protestants, in particular, as Hooker had recognised, had to contend with those who sought 'to draw all things unto the determination of bare and naked Scripture' until 'the name of the Light of Nature is made hateful with men; the *Star of Reason and Learning,* and all other such like helps, beginneth no otherwise to be thought of, than if it were an unlucky Comet . . .'[2] The Puritans of whom Hooker wrote were certainly among the most important detractors of learning that Bacon had in mind when he defended it in his *The Advancement of Learning* (1605).

Bacon's own solution rested on as rigid a separation as possible between religious and secular knowledge. From their admixture sprang errors in philosophy and heresies in religion. Hence, his detestation for the Platonism which tied natural phenomena to spiritual principles in an ascending hierarchy, and for the moderns who went 'so far as to found a system of natural philosophy on the first chapter of Genesis, or the book of Job, and other parts of the sacred writings, seeking the dead among the living . . .'[3] The same result, though in a different way, came from the schoolmen who reduced

---

[1] *The Laws of Ecclesiastical Polity* (London, 1682), p. 50.
[2] *Ibid.* p. 135.
[3] *Nov. Org.* (I, lxv), in *Works,* IV, p. 66.

theology to an art and incorporated into it 'the contentious and thorny philosophy of Aristotle', and thus 'to discourse of nature is made harder and more perilous ...'[1]

Bacon agreed with the Hermetics in believing that 'in this theatre of man's life it is reserved only for God and angels to be lookers on',[2] and that of all activities the study of nature for the glory of God and the benefit of man was noblest and was superior to the moral philosophy beloved of the humanists in being the 'great mother of all sciences'.[3] Reason by itself was an unsuitable instrument for penetrating the subtleties of nature. Man must approach nature in a spirit of patient humility rather than with the arrogant intellectual pride enshrined in Aristotle's system. He must observe and experiment, and give particular attention to the knowledge gained in the mechanical arts from 'vexed' nature. Attention has been focussed heretofore on 'the quiescent principles, *wherefrom*, and not the moving principles, *whereby*, things are produced', although 'the former tend to discourse, the latter to works'.[4]

At the same time, those noble ends must be purified of the 'vanity and superstition' with which the Hermetics had infected them.[5] A distrust of human reason did not sanction an uncritical resort to scripture or pretended illumination. The Hermetic insistence on experience and experiment in the study of nature had to be detached from its magical setting, which made it rather like incommunicable mystical experience. The search for particulars and specificity must be made systematic by applying the sort of procedures which the new centralised monarchies employed to sift information.[6] Bacon believed that the widespread longing for a natural philosophy less 'heathen' than Aristotle's was satisfied when it was dedicated to the twin ends of praising God through the study of His works and enriching man with discoveries and inventions. In a significantly amended version of Pico's famous description, Bacon remarked that the natural magic he sought to rehabilitate would, by applying 'the knowledge of hidden forms to the

[1] *Nov. Org.* (I, lxxxix), *Works,* IV, p. 88. [2] *Adv. Lear. Works,* III, p. 421.
[3] *Nov. Org.* (I, lxxix–lxxx), *Works,* IV, pp. 78–9.
[4] *Nov. Org.* (I, lxvi), *Works,* IV, p. 67. [5] *Adv. Lear. Works,* III, p. 351.
[6] *Nov. Org.* (I, xcviii), *Works,* IV, pp. 94–5.

production of wonderful operations, of uniting (as they say) actives with passives, displays the wonderful works of nature'.[1] These forms signified for him 'laws of action', the 'primary elements of nature; such as dense and rare, hot and cold, solid and fluid, heavy and light ...'[2] It was far more likely that such knowledge would one day make it possible to 'superinduce upon some metal the nature and form of gold ... than that some grains of the medicine projected should in a few moments of time turn a sea of quicksilver or some other material into gold ...'[3]

Despite Bacon's zeal to distinguish his own work sharply from the spirit and methods of the Hermetics, many of their ideas were reflected in his writings. He had ridiculed the alchemists for deriving chemical secrets from pagan myth; but his own works were pervaded by a belief in a pristine knowledge which he associated, above all, with Solomon, and he attempted to unveil natural secrets conveyed by the ancients in the guise of myth and parable.[4] In the natural histories which were to serve as the foundation of his physics, Bacon was forced to rely on authors like Pliny, Cardano, Paracelsus, and Porta.[5] To waste labour on the first principles of nature, whether elements or atoms, 'can do but little for the welfare of mankind',[6] and Bacon, therefore, had to resort a great deal to the 'spirits' which alchemists, natural magicians, and iatrochemists had discussed as the carriers of celestial powers. Finally, his *New Atlantis* (1627) bore great similarities to the Hermetic-utopian societies depicted in such works as J. V. Andreae's *Reipublicae Christianapolitanae descriptio* (1619) and Campanella's *De civita solis* (1623).

James I had remarked of the *Advancement of Learning*, which Bacon dedicated to him, that 'it is like the peace of God, that surpasseth all understanding'.[7] Bacon had confided to his

---

1 *De aug. sc.* IV, ch. 2, *Works*, IV, p. 379.
2 'The Plan of the Great Instauration', *Works*, IV, p. 29.
3 *Adv. Lear.* (bk. 2, VIII, 3), *Works*, III, p. 362.
4 *Adv. Lear. Works*, III, p. 298, pp. 448–52. C. W. Lemmi, *The Classical Deities in Bacon* (Baltimore, 1933); 'De principiis atque originibus' in *Works*, III, pp. 79–118; 'De sapientia Veterum' I, pp. 607–764.
5 Especially in *Sylva Sylvarum* (London, 1627); see J. R. Partington, *A History of Chemistry* (London, 1961); vol. II, p. 394.
6 *Nov. Org.* I, lxvii; *Works*, IV, p. 68.
7 Cited by I. D'Israeli, *Curiosities of Literature* (London, 1838), p. 492.

journal his isolation and lack of sympathetic patrons. His ideas on the reform of natural philosophy seem to have made little impact in England during his lifetime, and some years after his death his chaplain, William Rawley, wrote that 'his fame is greater and sounds louder in foreign parts than at home in his own nation . . .'[1]

The great revival of Bacon's ideals and programme took place in England just before and during the period of the civil wars and the Commonwealth, under the aegis at first, ironically, of those who sought to assimilate them with the Hermeticism which Bacon had set out to purify. They regarded a 'Christian' natural philosophy as part of much greater reform which would build a new Jerusalem. England became the focus of the hopes of various European thinkers as their own lands were devastated by the Thirty Years' War. They recognised a kindred spirit in the writings of Bacon. Comenius narrated in 1641 that when he first read Bacon's *Instauratio magna* he saw it as heralding 'a new age of philosophers'.[2] But Comenius sought a reformation without tarrying and complained that Bacon had furnished the 'true key of nature' but left the creation of a true body of knowledge to the industry of several generations of observations and inductions. Comenius argued that where sense and reason proved impotent, there scripture must be brought in to supply the deficiencies. He himself derived the basic principles from an interpretation of the text of *Genesis*, and tried to explain nature in terms of three principles which corresponded at one level to the Trinity, at another to the Paracelsian *tria prima*.[3] A true body of natural knowledge could then be built upon them and incorporated within an encyclopaedic system which Comenius believed could be taught to everyone, even 'men of the lowest rank, condemned to labour and grievous troubles . . .'[4]

The ideals of the continental reformers were broadcast in England by the group around the Palatinate refugee Samuel Hartlib who lived in England from 1628 until his death in

[1] 'Life' in *Works*, I, p. 15.
[2] *Physicae ad lumen divinum synopsis* (Leipzig, 1933); cited from preface in Eng. tr. of London, 1651.
[3] *Ibid.*
[4] *A Pattern of Universall Knowledge* (London, 1651), p. 25, Eng. tr. of *Pansophiae diatyposis* (Danzig, 1643).

1662.[1] They became potent in the climate of hope for far-reaching changes in church and society which was ushered in by the Long Parliament of 1640, summoned by Charles I because of financial exigencies. John Pym, the leader of the reforming party, was a supporter of Hartlib. In 1641, when chiliastic hopes were widely nursed, Hartlib invited Comenius to England with the support of influential Parliamentarians, in order to establish Bacon's 'Salomon's House'. Although the outbreak of the civil war compelled Comenius to leave, the Hartlib group continued to bombard Parliament with proposals for comprehensive educational and social reform. Its influence on Robert Boyle is especially worth examining as, next to Bacon, Boyle may seem best to exemplify the Puritan–science connection.

Boyle, a younger son of the first Earl of Cork, received his private education on the continent with a tutor. In 1638, in Calvin's Geneva, Boyle experienced what he later called the 'considerablest' event in his whole life – when he was only twelve. A violent thunderstorm at night seemed to him like the end of the world described in the Apocalypse, and he found himself unprepared for the Day of Judgement.[2] A similar event in the life of Martin Luther had impelled him to take the vow to become a monk. Boyle pledged himself, if he was spared, to a life which would be 'more religiously and carefully employed'. His religious turmoil is indicated by his confessing that when he visited Grenoble a little later, the devil put into his mind 'hideous thoughts' and 'distracting doubts of some of the fundamentals of Christianity'.

Returning in 1644 to an England in the throes of civil war, he soon came in touch with the Hartlib group, probably through his sister, Lady Ranelagh, who was their great patroness. There was no irony in Boyle's remark in a letter to his former tutor in 1646 that he was studying 'natural philosophy, the mechanics, and husbandry according to the principle of our new philosophical college, that values no knowledge but

---

[1] G. H. Turnbull, *Samuel Hartlib* (Oxford, 1920); *Hartlib, Dury and Comenius* (London, 1947); H. R. Trevor-Roper, 'The Three Foreigners : The Philosophers of the Puritan Revolution', in *Religion, the Reformation and Social Change* (London, 1967), pp. 237–93, and C. Webster, introd. to his *Samuel Hartlib and the Advancement of Learning* (Cambridge, 1970), pp. 1–72.

[2] *Works*, ed. T. Birch (London, 1744), I, p. 12.

as it hath a tendency to use'.[1] The next year he enthusiastically approved Hartlib's plan for having Campanella's *City of the Sun* and Andreae's *Christianapolis* translated into English, since they deserved 'to be taught in our language'.[2]

Boyle's interest in what had become the science *par excellence* of the Hermetics, chemistry, is evident soon after he settled at his Dorset manor of Stalbridge (1645–52), where he was visited by the members of that 'Invisible College' whose universal charity made them 'take the whole body of mankind for their care'.[3] He knew the chemists in the Hartlib circle. In 1648 he described how 'by the help of anatomical knives and the light of chemical furnaces, I study the book of nature consult the glosses of Aristotle, Epicurus, Paracelsus, Harvey, Helmont, and other learned expositors of that instructive volume'.[4] He wrote on ethical and religious as well as scientific topics, both at Stalbridge and while on his father's estates in Ireland. What must undoubtedly be an early letter to Hartlib well illustrates his views at this time. Boyle thought that the great deal of attention given to observational astronomy could be justified only if it produced benefits or use for human advantage, otherwise 'we know them only to know them'.[5] He believed that such a defence was possible, and couched it in terms of ideas of celestial spirits acting on man's sidereal or astral body which could have come out of Ficino or Paracelsus. In keeping with the Hartlib group's interests, Boyle foresaw great advantages from such studies as 'husbandry, in gardens, in physick, and to the producing of many other very stupendous effects'.

The contrast between these views and those of his later years are so striking that a decisive break with the 'Baconianism' of the Hartlib group at some stage must be supposed. It occurred at a time of moderate reaction against the Hermetic natural philosophy as it began to be identified with the more extreme sectarians.[6] With the overthrow of monarchy and

[1] *Ibid.* I, p. 20.
[2] Letter of 8 April 1647, cited by G. H. Turnbull, 'John Hall's Letters to Samuel Hartlib', *Review of English Studies*, n.s. IV (1953), 221-33.
[3] *Works*, I, p. 20.   [4] See note 2, p. 19 above.
[5] Title xiii in 'The General History of the Air' (1692), in *Works*, v, pp. 124–8.
[6] P. M. Rattansi, 'Paracelsus and the Puritan Revolution', *Ambix*, XI (1963), 24–32.

divisions among the victorious party, the growth of sects recruiting their members from the lower classes appeared the greatest menace to the re-establishment of social stability. Already in 1641 Lord Brooke had sympathetically described how the popular tub-thumpers expected a pouring out of God's spirit on all flesh 'till Knowledge cover the Earth, as Waters fill the Sea ... and they poore men expect a new Heaven, and a new Earth, wherein there shall neede no more Temples of stone, but all good men shall be Prophets, Priests, and Kings'.[1] In the same year John Milton had called out: 'Come forth out of thy Royall chambers, O Prince of all the Kings of the earth ... for now: all creatures sigh to bee renewed.'[2] By 1646 Boyle indicated his alarm at the danger of sectaries in London, holding 'no less than 200 several opinions on points of religion', and feared their disputes would bring religion itself into disrepute.[3]

Reading Bacon in the period of moderate reaction against the sectarians, Boyle could find in it an alternative to the enchanted natural philosophy of the sectarians, and a compromise between his early hope of discharging a religious obligation by using science for human welfare and his enhanced sensitivity to the intimate ties which linked Hermetic and Paracelsian science with the radicals he thought would destroy the existing social order. He was able to take Bacon's programme even farther and free it from a residual animism because he could draw upon a mechanical conception of nature which had been developed in a systematic and coherent form during this period by Descartes and Gassendi.

Like Bacon, Boyle believed that man must recover the power over brute creation with which he had aboriginally been endowed. By relentlessly drawing out the implications of the mechanical concept, he endowed this ideal with a new meaning. Nature was stripped of life and sense and reduced to a dead and 'admirably contriv'd automaton'.[4] Awe, veneration, or a sympathetic understanding of the sort urged by the Hermetics was grotesquely inappropriate when

---

[1] W. Haller, *The Rise of Puritanism* (New York, 1957 ed.), p. 338.
[2] *Ibid.* p. 357.
[3] Letters of 1646 and 1647 in *Works*, I, p. 19, p. 21, p. 23.
[4] *Works*, IV, p. 417.

inspecting a dead if highly ingenious artifact. The advantages were twofold. Nothing need deter man from reassuming that power over creation which David had described in Psalm VIII: 'Thou madest him to have dominion over the works of thine hands, and hast put all things under his feet.' For the personification of nature had 'obstructed and confined the empire of man over the inferior creatures'.[1] Moreover, admiration would then be directed to the author of nature, rather than 'looking upon merely corporeal, and often inanimate things as endowed with life, sense, and understanding', which lay at the root of pagan polytheism and idolatry. The mechanical conception was therefore a far more religious one than that commonly received. Nature in the raw – the wild mountains at Grenoble, for example – had induced gloomy and hideous thoughts in Boyle's mind. He admired in it what he could regard as analogous to human artifacts, seeing in animals, plants, and human bodies infinitely more subtle and ingenious 'Strasburg clocks'.

So extreme was Boyle's rejection of animism that he condemned the idea of laws of nature since they seemed to endow dead matter with the ability to comprehend and obey divine commands.[2] But he wished to retain man at the centre of creation, and he criticised Descartes' ironical reflection that man, occupying a small portion of an unimportant planet, should believe that God had hung sun and moon in the sky for his benefit. Patient study was likely to enable man to gain a far larger share of his patrimony than aiming at immediate usefulness. Bacon had advised the natural philosopher to concentrate at first on experiments of light, and only later on those of fruit, thus emulating God, who created light on the first day and works on subsequent ones. Boyle, too, now distinguished sharply between those who 'care only to know nature' and those who 'desire to command her'.[3] The latter sort may seem to have endowed mankind with many useful inventions: Paracelsus had probably never heard of atomical notions, yet 'was able to perform some things that were truly admirable ...' However, when experimental

[1] *Ibid.* IV, p. 363.
[2] *Works*, IV, pp. 521, 531.
[3] *Ibid.* I, p. 199.

natural philosophy was sufficiently advanced, it would bring far more benefit to human life and be freed 'from all imputation of barrenness'.

Though convinced that to be truly intelligible scientific explanations must be couched in mechanical terms, Boyle introduced a cautious Baconian empiricism into the continental mechanical philosophy and was critical of what he regarded as the premature system-building of Descartes. He accepted the Baconian programme of a patient study of 'forms' such as fluidity and solidity, heat and cold, but could now attribute these much more consistently to the configuration and motion of the small parts of bodies. Bacon had hoped that a knowledge of 'forms' would make it possible to 'superinduce' them on any piece of matter. Boyle accepted the possibility of such a reformed alchemy, and it was the basis of what has been well described as 'his novel conception of the chemist as an artificer who fabricates in the microscopic realm as the mechanic does in the macroscopic'.[1] The Hermetic conception of a universal science of chemistry was now to be realised in mechanical terms.

Man engaged in the 'philosophical worship' of God by studying the dead and inert universe of matter, which owed all activity to the motion impressed on its parts at Creation by God. Attention was to be directed primarily to structure and configuration, and the role of such agencies as the world-soul or the *spiritus* was of little concern to the natural philosopher. The notion of forces, over and above matter and motion, seemed as animistic to Boyle as it had to Descartes. To count as scientific, an explanation must be couched in mechanical terms, and it mattered little whether the origins of motion were located in such general principles as the *materia subtilis* of Descartes, the *anima mundi* of the Platonists, or the 'Universal Spirit' of the chemists.[2]

Far more faithful to Renaissance Platonism were the contemporary English thinkers usually described as the Cambridge Platonists. Their motives for enthusiastically embracing the basic mechanical concept of Descartes were

---

[1] T. S. Kuhn, 'Boyle and Structural Chemistry in the Seventeenth Century', *Isis*, XXXXIII (1932), 31.
[2] *Works*, III, p. 453.

fundamentally religious. They believed that religion was menaced from two contrary directions in the chaos of civil war. First, from a resurgence of 'atheism', now particularly perilous since it had spread to the lower classes, and owing much to the purer Aristotelianism of such Italian thinkers as Pomponazzi and Cesalpino.[1] The other danger came (as Boyle had come to fear) from the sectaries who grounded every heresy on the claim of private inspiration, and who derived much support from the Hermetics, especially Paracelsus.[2] The Cartesian philosophy, which was really the restoration of a pristine Mosaic system of knowledge, rescued religion from these twin dangers.[3] It furnished a natural philosophy as rational and intellectually coherent as Aristotle's, but far more religious in spirit and supporting basic Christian tenets, thus repairing that deficiency in positive knowledge which had plagued all previous attempts to re-establish the Platonic philosophy. It exposed the confused and superstitious character of the doctrines expounded by the Hermetics and their sectarian allies. The Cartesian system appeared undeniably Platonic to the Cambridge thinkers. It accepted innate ideas. By conceiving matter as dead and inert, it located the origin of all power and activity in the spiritual realm.

But the Cambridge Platonists made an extremely important reservation about the mechanical conception which neither Descartes nor Boyle found acceptable, but which was destined to influence Isaac Newton's philosophy of nature in a fundamental manner. The dead and inert character of matter pointed to the absolute necessity of a spiritual factor not merely in the beginning, at Creation, but at all times. When any natural phenomenon was traced far enough, the analysis would reveal gaps in the chain of mechanical causality which could only be bridged by invoking 'incorporeal' principles not reducible to matter and motion.[4] The intervention of God – or

---

[1] Some aspects of the mortalist controversy are discussed by G. Williamson, 'Milton and the Mortalist Heresy', in his *Seventeenth Century Contexts* (London, 1960), pp. 148–77.

[2] Rattansi, *op. cit.* pp. 29–30.

[3] Henry More, *A Collection of Several Philosophical Writings* (London, 1662), Preface general, pp. xvii–xix; 'An Appendix to the Defence of the Philosophick Cabbala', pp. 103–4.

[4] 'An Antidote Against Atheism' (1652) in *ibid.* esp. pp. 38–47; also *Remarks Upon Two late Ingenious Discourses* (London, 1676).

rather of his subordinate agency – was continually necessary, for the mere operation of mechanical laws would soon dissolve the world into chaos. That subordinate agency was the 'hylarchic' principle, or the 'plastic spirit', a re-statement of the neo-Platonic world-soul. But it was freed from astrological ideas and the possibilities of using it for magical benefits were firmly discounted. The goal of knowledge, in any case, was understanding, not power in the vulgar Baconian or Hermetic manner. The worth of a philosophy, as More tartly remarked in 1649, was not to be measured by 'what help it can procure for ye back, bed, and board'.[1] In a host of phenomena – in gravitation, cohesion, electrical and magnetic action, in the very notions of space and extension – the Cambridge thinkers pointed to the limitations of the mechanical philosophy and the necessity for an incorporeal principle in the structure of any satisfactory explanation.

Views similar in many ways to those of Henry More were held by Richard Baxter (1615–91), who has proved a rich source for Max Weber's Protestantism–capitalism and Merton's Puritanism–science theses. Like More, he had refuted those who doubted the immortality of the human soul, and pointed to the connection between the extreme sectaries who had 'filled with blood' many countries of Europe and the ideas of Paracelsus.[2] He opposed fundamentalists, saying: 'I would not Christians take up with Scripture-wisdom only, without studying Philosophy and other Heathens Humane Learning ...'[3] Of such studies, 'physical Phylosophy is nothing but the Knowledge of Gods Works' and especially to be commended. But it was 'one thing to know Gods Works and God in them, and another thing to compose a systeme of Physicks and with a great many Uncertainties and Untruths ...' In a comprehensive review of ancient and modern natural philosophers, he found all defective, including the 'Hermetical Philosophers' who lacked true method and formed a system of philosophy from three or five principles. On corpuscular and mechanical notions, his judgement was:

[1] C. Webster, 'Henry More and Descartes: Some New Sources', *Brit. J. Hist. Sci.*, IV (1969), 359–77 (p. 368).
[2] 'A Christian Directory' (written 1664–5), in *Practical Works* (London, 1707), vol. I, p. 51; *ibid.* II, p. 320.
[3] *Ibid.* I, p. 708.

P. M. Rattansi

The Epicureans or Democritists were still and justly the contempt of all the sober sects; and our late Somatists that follow them, yea and *Gassendus*, and many that call themselves Cartesians, yea *Cartesius* himself, much more *Berigardius*, *Regius*, *Hobbes*, doe give so much more to meer Matter and Motion, than is truly due, and know or say so much too little of Spirits, active Natures, Vital Powers, which are the true principles of motion, that they differ as much from true Philosophers, as a Carcas or a Clock from a living man.[1]

Baxter's advice to students, therefore, was to 'join together the study of Physicks and Theology; and take not your Physicks separated from or independent of Theology'. Also: 'And study not the doctrine of *Bodies* alone, as separated from Spirits: For it is but an imaginary separation, and a delusion to men's minds. Or if you will *call them* by the name of *several Sciences*, be sure you so link these severalls together that the due dependence of Bodies on Spirits, and of the Passive nature on the Active may still be kept discernible: And then they will *be one* while you call *them divers* . . .'

Baxter's reference to Thomas Hobbes and the modern 'Somatists' (or Mortalists) shows the fears that the publication of Hobbes' mechanical materialism had aroused: that a self-sufficient mechanical explanation, even when acknowledging God's agency at Creation, could become a far more insidious threat to the religious picture of the world than 'Averroist' Aristotelians. His division of bodies and spirits into passives and actives follows the Cambridge Platonist account. His final assessment of natural philosophy was that 'the Philosophers are still in very great darkness, and there is much confusion, defectiveness, division and uncertainty among them', and all that was possible was to select so much of the *'Certainties* and *useful* parts of Physicks' as possible, and ignore their controversies.

It was in this atmosphere of disillusionment with the religious implications of the mechanical philosophy and an insistence on its incompleteness unless joined with active and incorporeal principles that Newton's own intellectual formation took shape.[2] It furnished a metaphysical support for his notion of a variety of forces to infuse life and activity into a dead and

---

[1] *Ibid.* I, p. 715; *ibid.* II, pp. 165–224 and Boyle, *Works*, v, pp. 552–5.
[2] Esp. in 'De gravitatione', A. R. & M. B. Hall, eds., *Unpublished Scientific Papers of Isaac Newton* (Cambridge, 1962), pp. 89–156.

inert world of matter where motion ever tended towards diminution and all natural processes towards extinction.[1] A combination of the Renaissance dynamical conception and of the mechanical philosophy, both in a modified English adaption, may in an important sense be said to underlie his enormous achievement in quantifying one of these forces, the gravitational attraction that bound together the 'System of the World'. While he rejected the intermediary 'Hylarchic Principle' of the Cambridge Platonists and wished to attribute causality far more immediately to the ever-present activity of God, tracing His continual agency in the universe led Newton into the labyrinth of alchemy and into the study of the prefiguring of the true system of the world which, in the spirit of the Florentine and Cambridge Platonists, he located in ancient natural philosophy.[2] In the historical perspective sketched above, it is possible to realise that these aspects of his total world-picture need not be regarded as embarrassments which require elaborate psychological explanations. The social, religious, and pedagogic reform with which these tendencies had come to be associated in the post-Reformation era almost disappeared in the Cambridge Platonist formulation which so strongly influenced Newton's own approach.

IV

The study of nature by rational-experimental means to gratify the twin ends of glorifying God and making discoveries for human benefit is to be regarded, then, not so much as an English Puritan belief but rather as a mainly Protestant sixteenth-century ideal which was taken over and 'purified' by Francis Bacon, although it attained little influence in England during his own life-time. A combination of circumstances gave it great prominence during the 1640–60 period. There was the influence of the Hartlib–Dury–Comenius group, whose ideas fitted into the plans of social and educational reform entertained by the leadership in the Long Parliament. By the late

[1] *Opticks*, Query 31 of 1730 London ed. (New York, 1952), pp. 397–400.
[2] J. E. McGuire & P. M. Rattansi, 'Newton and the "Pipes of Pan"', *Notes & Records of the Royal Society of London*, XXI (1966), 108–43.

1640s, the mechanical conception of Descartes and Gassendi had an enormous intellectual impact, not least because it appeared a serviceable weapon for defending religion simultaneously against Hermetic sectaries and mortalists.

At the Restoration, some of the religious-utilitarian ideal of science survived in the newly-founded Royal Society, wedded now on the whole to Baconian-mechanical science. But the upper-class patronage of 'new science', which was partly a fashion which had influenced Charles II during his exile in France, soon declined, and the leading figures during the rest of the century were those recruited during the revolutionary period. Sixteenth-century Hermetics, as well as the major figures of the seventeenth-century scientific movement like Bacon, Descartes, and Boyle were committed to an evaluation of the study of nature as the noblest of all studies and basic to all programmes of a reformed education. The weakening and disintegration of this vision of 'new science' can already be detected in the 1650s in England, and it continued throughout the post-Restoration period, without having resulted in the creation of institutional arrangements of sufficient significance to render it less dependent on the accidents of patronage or the vagaries of fashion.

Refuting the sectaries who wished the English universities to lay aside their disputations 'and betake our selves, to Agriculture, Mechanicks, Chymistry and the like' by the light of the works of Paracelsus, Helmont and Fludd, two leading members of the Oxford group of young natural philosophers asked in 1654 which of the nobility or gentry desired that when they sent their sons to the universities. They wanted their sons to 'become Rationall and Graceful speakers, and be of an acceptable behaviour in their Countries'.[1] In the reaffirmation of education as the intellectual formation of the courtier, there was little place for scientific studies. If the gentleman was to make himself useful to society, why should he spend much time on natural philosophy, which had singularly failed to produce the material plenty promised by Bacon, nor conferred the intellectual satisfaction of any certainty in its conclusions, as was freely confessed by mechanical philosophers like Robert Boyle?

[1] John Wilkins & Seth Ward, *Vindiciae Academiarum* (Oxford, 1654), p. 50.

A whole stream of literary works and satires on the Royal Society throughout the post-Restoration period urged that literature and moral philosophy were the proper concerns of gentlemen, rather than natural philosophy. Meric Casaubon complained in 1669:

> truly I think that they do not go a right way, either to improve the *Glory of God*, or humane wisdom, who do magnifie this study, as though there were no other wisdom in the world to be thought of, or pursued after; that make it the onely, *useful*, true solid learning, to which they would have all Schools and Universities fitted, and to which the Nobility of the land are invited, as to the employment of all employments the most worthy of their entertainment.[1]

Henry Stubbe testily observed: 'It was not intended of the *Virtuosi:* "Except ye become like these, ye shall not enter... Heaven."'[2] Others complained about the uncertainty of scientific conjectures. Samuel Butler scoffed that the natural philosophers judged nature as the rabble did affairs of State: 'They see things done, and every Man according to his Capacity guesses at the Reasons of them, but knowing nothing of the Arcana or secret Movements of either, they seldom or never are in the Right.'[3] Even John Locke, in the *Essay*, concluded that human senses could not penetrate to the insensible particles of bodies, and by observing their 'Figure, Size, Connexion, and Motion' tell why rhubarb purged, hemlock killed, and opium made a man sleep, 'how far soever humane Industry may advance useful and experimental Philosophy *in physical Things*, scientifical will still be out of our reach'.[4] While he did not wish to 'dis-esteem, or *dissuade the Study of Nature*', the conclusion was inescapable that if natural philosophy could never be made a science, while morality was demonstrable, '*Morality* is *the proper Science, and Business of Mankind in general*.'[5]

Would it be possible to detect 'Puritan' values in Bacon's purification of Hermeticism, since Max Weber regarded

---

[1] *A letter of Meric Casaubon, D. D. &c. To Peter du Moulin D.D. and Prebendarie of the same Church: Concerning Natural experimental Philosophie, and some books lately set out about it* (Cambridge, 1669), p. 24.

[2] *A Censure upon... the History of the Royal Society* (London, 1670).

[3] 'A Philosopher' in 'Characters' ('chiefly drawn up from 1667 to 1669'), in *The Genuine Remains* (London, 1759), vol. II, p. 129.

[4] *An Essay concerning Humane Understanding* (London, 1690), p. 278.

[5] *Ibid.* p. 327.

Puritanism as a great agency in the disenchantment of the world? There is some plausibility in the suggestion; but the quest for order and disenchantment after a long period of crisis in almost every sphere of life was a general feature of the European intellectual landscape in the late sixteenth and early seventeenth centuries.[1] Not merely the Protestant Thomas Erastus,[2] but the Catholic Mersenne[3] and Descartes were as concerned as Bacon to counter Hermeticism as a 'sect-type' ideology, which struck a responsive chord most often among the most radical wing of the Reformation.

The historical background sketched in the preceding sections should also indicate the crudity of the distinction between 'internal' and 'external' factors when applied to this period in the history of science. What Bacon called the study of nature 'with a view to works' was tied until the early modern period to a preference for a neo-Platonic framework of ideas. This was far more congenial to concentration on the prodigious and marvellous in nature – aimed at producing such effects by human effort – than the sober naturalism of the Aristotelian system. In the thirteenth century St Thomas Aquinas attempted to discourage such ideas, in the spirit of Aristotle, by a classical distinction between the ordinary course of nature and the divine and demonic interventions a Christian must accept.[4] The continuing importance of these ideas, through Arabic authors like Al-Kindi, in the complex atmosphere of doubt and scepticism in the fourteenth and fifteenth centuries, is shown by the pains taken by such a defender of the Aristotelian tradition as Nicolas Oresme to explain *mirabilia* and such 'occult' effects as magnetism, the echenis fish, and the power of music by a doctrine of the 'configuration of qualities' which would minimise the importance of celestial influences or incorporeal spirits.[5] Roger Bacon, himself

---

1 Cf. R. Mousnier, *Les xvie et xviie siècles* (Paris, 1961), esp. pp. 161–363.
2 Discussed in Pagel, *Paracelsus*, pp. 311–33.
3 See R. Lenoble, *Mersenne ou la naissance du mécanisme* (Paris, 1943).
4 In *Summa Contra Gentiles*, Bk. 3, pt. 2, Chs. CI–CVIII; compare Bacon: 'from the wonders of nature is the nearest intelligence and passage towards the wonders of art: for it is no more but by following, and as it were hounding nature in her wanderings [from her usual course], to be able to lead her afterwards to the same place again'.
5 M. Clagett, ed. & tr., *Nicole Oresme and the Medieval Geometry of Qualities and Motions* (Madison, Milwaukee, & London, 1968).

inclined towards 'operative natural philosophy', explained occult effects through his doctrine of the 'multiplication of species'.[1] In the same period, the neo-Platonic idea of the *spiritus* formed the background to a striking success in the development of alchemical distillation techniques for medical purposes by John of Rupescissa, the Joachimite Franciscan.[2]

As we saw above, just as neo-Platonism helped to legitimate the Renaissance delight in the flesh and the beauty of the natural world in the trans-Alpine lands, so too the dream of greatly enhancing human power over nature to cure diseases and prolong life, expand agricultural and horticultural production, and (to a lesser extent) devise machines to augment human labour took shape mainly in a neo-Platonic or Hermetic framework. The reaction of the 'internal' tradition is noticeable especially in the purer Aristotelianism of the Paduan thinkers, from Pomponazzi[3] to Fracastoro,[4] and their explanations of prodigies often moved perilously close to atomic or corpuscular notions. But to return to the pure doctrines of Aristotle, in reaction to Hermeticism, was to court the opposite danger for Christian belief, since it would result in explaining away not merely the prodigious and demonic but also the miraculous in naturalistic fashion. Mersenne was aware of that danger, as had been Erastus who, a little earlier, had made little distinction between the doctrines of Pomponazzi and of Paracelsus. The mechanical concept seemed initially to avoid both dangers and that provided an important religious motive for its systematic articulation for both Mersenne and Descartes. The explanation of *mirabilia* – echenis fish and all – can be found in such a late example as Pierre Gassendi's *Syntagma philosophicum* (1658), now in mechanical and corpuscular terms.[5]

Lastly, in understanding the formation of Newton's world-

---

[1] *De Spiecierum Multiplicatione* (Frankfurt 1614 ed.)

[2] L. Thorndike, *A History of Magic and Experimental Science* (New York, 1934), vol. III, pp. 347–69; R. P. Multhauf, 'John of Rupescissa and the origin of medical chemistry', *Isis*, XXXXIV (1954), 359–67. See also F. Sherwood Taylor, *The Alchemists* (1949) (New York, 1962), pp. 93–101.

[3] *De naturalium effectuum causis, sive de incantationibus* (written 1520, Basel, 1556).

[4] Girolamo Fracastoro, *De sympathia et antipathium rerum* (Venice, 1546).

[5] *Opera Omnia* (Lugduni-Anisson & Devenet, 1658), vol. I, pt. 2, sec. I, bk. 6, 'de qualitatibus rerum'; compare W. Charleton, *Philosophia Epicuro–Gassendo–Charltoniana* (London, 1654) pp. 341–413.

view, the modification of the continental mechanical philosophy in England, during the contingencies of the revolutionary period, has fully to be taken into account and eludes any neat separation of 'internal' and 'external' factors. The failure to appreciate that lies at the root of many stubborn puzzles about Newton's ideas and pre-occupations.

If there is a 'solid, if elusive, core of truth'[1] in the Merton thesis, as there may be in the larger Weber thesis, then it will have to be established by future research which must be far more sensitive to the continually changing character of the science and the society whose interaction it studies. It certainly cannot satisfactorily be pursued by isolating England from the much larger world of European learning of which it formed a part. These are only some of the formidable problems in an area of historical studies which poses a new challenge to historians.

[1] H. R. Trevor-Roper, *op. cit.* p. 6.

2

SCIENCE, TECHNOLOGY AND UTOPIA IN THE SEVENTEENTH CENTURY

by A. Rupert Hall

There has long been a verbal association between *science* and *Utopia*, and again between the words *technology* and *Utopia*. Ideal societies have rarely been imagined as ignorant and primitive. Yet it would be wrong to assume from this double association that, even in relation to the idea of Utopia, science and technology are virtually synonymous or at least equivalent terms; they are in truth as disparate as deduction and induction, as socialism and capitalism, or one might better say thought and action, since science is (roughly speaking) knowledge of our natural environment, while technology is the exercise of a working control over it. Scientific knowledge may be of many kinds: for example it may be the descriptive, enumerative type of knowledge by which one species of fish is distinguished from another, or knowledge of a speculative character by which we try to account for the appearance of the cosmos. Two of the very obvious drives in the development of scientific research have been this former one, of an acquisitive character, towards enumerating, collecting, describing and classifying things, and this latter one, of a philosophic character, towards providing rational accounts of our experience.

We insist thus upon the obvious simply in order to make it clearer that there have been in the past very large areas of scientific activity that have in principle, and not merely by accident or imperfection, no part in that knowledge which is called useful because it helps man to master nature through technology, or the crafts. Neither enumeration nor explanation is logically connected by necessity with control. So the type of scientific activity that is directed by considerations of utility is a third species, and not always the most important one. Even today, when vast sums of money are directed into utilitarian scientific research, the two biggest sinks of national wealth (at least in the USA and the USSR) are projects motivated by considerations of national prestige rather than by those of scientific rationality or utility to mankind.

Another general distinction which should be drawn is this. In so far as the satisfactions obtained from scientific work are intellectual they are immediately realisable; one's success is proportionate to one's skill in enumerating and describing, or in devising an acceptable theoretical explanation, within the context of the science of one's time. One sets one's own objective, and the standards of success in attaining it are known. If a zoologist makes a catalogue of all the species of spiders in Cambridgeshire he is not to be blamed for omitting the species of worms; whereas a farmer might be just as much interested in the worms in his fields, as in the spiders. Similarly with a theory; our reasons for believing a theory to hold good are quite distinct from the question of its technological applicability, and always have been. For instance, we do not at the present time regard our whole theory of electrochemistry as false and useless because it does not teach us how to construct an electric storage battery with a capacity of (say) 500 watt/hours per pound weight, which would be a fantastically useful device. So in exactly the same way people in the seventeenth century did not suppose their medical ideas to be false because medicine in practice could not prevent their children from dying of common and easily contracted diseases. One's ideas about the nature of the world, and how one would make the world different if one could, are not by any means in a simple correspondence.

To my mind, the belief that we climb up to heaven by mounting a ladder called SCIENCE, which conducts us to a second ladder called TECHNICAL PROFICIENCY, which in turn brings us to UTOPIA, is an essentially modern belief. One need hardly draw attention to its inherent crudity or to the modernity of its premises concerning material progress and the relative insignificance of the religious, moral and social state of humanity. Surely any historical perspective must make it clear that before the twentieth century the amelioration of society was seen as above all a moral or human problem, not a technical one, just as education was seen as a moral or humanising process and not as the inculcation of a variety of technical skills. Marxism and evangelical Christianity were at one in this, in visualising the millennium as consisting of a new system of human relationships and values – the one ethical, of course, the other social and economic. Marx was perfectly well aware that it was not by scientific or technical accomplishment that a capitalist and a communist society were to be distinguished. Scientists, until the later part of the nineteenth century, shared this universal opinion. Hitherto the men who followed science at all had done so either for the sake of its personal intellectual satisfactions or as an element in an educational scheme that was not directed towards technical or professional training (here, however, medicine should be seen as an exception). Hence they had no more need to justify science than, say, writing poetry or fox-hunting. They could and commonly did regard their work as useful because it contributed to the common stock of human knowledge, but no one bothered to analyse this complacency profoundly; certainly no one doubted that it was perfectly appropriate to both the study of the theory of numbers and the collection of fossils, however remote and unappealing such pursuits might appear to most people. In the late eighteenth century there were of course already instances of manufacturers consulting natural philosophers like Joseph Black, hoping for information that would make some process feasible; the philosopher was willing to impart such knowledge as he had, and was sometimes flattered by the consultation, but would never have imagined that the main justification of his work was its utility to manufacturers. And, in the same age, it was equally the case that no one doubted that the progress of technology was the business of such manufacturers and craftsmen. A clergyman inventor, a gentleman inventor, though there were indeed such, was an eccentric. In the language of the eighteenth century natural philosophy grew by increasing knowledge, invention sprang from ingenuity.

Therefore in the seventeenth century one must, in the first place, be careful not to start from notions about science and its relation to techniques that have grown up almost within living memory. One must also be careful with words like 'nse' and 'improvement' which are capable of having more than one significance.

It is well known that the flowering of English science in the late seventeenth century came after the founding of the Royal Society following upon the Restoration, an event which occurred when Newton was only eighteen, and Edmond Halley four, while all the younger Newtonians were still unborn. But obviously the seed that then flowered was planted much earlier and many who contributed to the Royal Society's great distinction (Boyle, Ray, Willis, Wallis, Lower, Hooke, Oldenburg and so on) were mature men when the Restoration took place. Hence it has long seemed natural to associate the scientific movement, so far as England is concerned, with the religious and political revolutions occurring simultaneously, even though strictly out of phase with these. Both forms of revolution aimed at bringing into existence a 'better England' (or Britain), and it can be argued that this was the object of the scientists also. (It should be obvious without more ado and without any argument that 'better' here means three different things at least.) However, the revolutionary movements that achieved most success, albeit temporary – the Independency in religion, and the rule of the army in politics – were not unique, and so one can look for other affiliations between the spirit of scientific revolution and these other, less successful progressive movements.

I shall not touch on religion, nor on politics, nor on these movements – like the Levellers or Harington's republican club – that seem to have little relation to science, education, or technology. I will begin with an educational and social reformer named Samuel Hartlib who had a considerable influence in England under the Commonwealth and Protectorate, and about whom quite a lot is now known because by some odd chance a great mass of his correspondence and other papers have survived, and are now in Sheffield. Hartlib was born at Elbing in Germany, coming to settle in England in 1628, when he was perhaps twenty-five or thirty years old, for he had studied at Cambridge only a few years before. Now the fact that Hartlib – and an associate of his by name Theodore Haak – was a German is significant, not only because he was one of the relatively few inhabitants of London who were directly in touch with the German Protestant cause during the Thirty Years' War, nor only because he had the similar unique distinction of communicating with intellectuals in Germany, but because he was (in particular) closely in touch with, and sympathetic towards, the German school of practitioners of esoteric or Hermetic arts, of which more later. We can formally claim that Hartlib was a Utopist since he published in 1641 *A Description of the famous Kingdom of Macaria*, a short and incoherent dialogue between a Scholar and the inevitable Traveller to strange lands. Hartlib's notion seems to be – the thing is very sketchy – that since men are naturally good, enlightened self-interest will secure the welfare of all. Macaria is governed by a supreme council under which are five subordinate economic councils (for agriculture, fishing, sea-trade, land-trade and colonies) which make wise rules for the normal activities of men, for example regulating the number of apprentices in a craft; there are apparently no professional men, rentiers or soldiers in Macaria. The main cause of the country's excellence in all arts is that: 'Any Experiment, for the Health or Wealth of Man [is] honourably rewarded at the public charge, by which their skill in husbandry, physic and surgery is most excellent.' To settle questions of opinion debates are held before the national Council, like medieval disputations, to decide what views are correct; teaching views or theories not approved in this way is punishable by death.

At the end there is some puffing discussion of a 'book of husbandry' written by the author, of which it is remarked 'no business can be of more weight than this, wherein the public good is so greatly furthered; which to further we are all bound by the law of God and Nature'.

Perhaps my summary has exaggerated the importance of Hartlib's point that technical ingenuity – not, be it noted, science – should be publicly rewarded. For the most part the merits of Macaria are supposed to rest on those old expedients, wise laws, military supremacy, social justice, and the calling to account of those responsible for administration before philosopher–kings. It does not seem to me that Hartlib's was a technological Utopia.

In fact he cherished such schemes to the end of his life,

37

his last hopes for their realisation being removed by the restoration of the monarchy. Antilia, as the proposed new community was called, was variously to be established in Poland, or in Virginia. We know little about the proposed structure of this ideal society, except that it was to be 'universal' (that is, Protestant, for non-Christians and Papists were excluded) and that it almost certainly involved the following elements: a reformed conduct of the Christian life; a reformed system of education and a means of disseminating useful knowledge. Hartlib wrote to Boyle of the objects of the community as being 'propagating religion and endeavouring the reformation of the whole world'. There is no suggestion at all that it contained any scientific-fiction element of technical marvels. And this view is confirmed by Hartlib's own repeated statement that, in his ideal commonwealth, he was in effect revising the schemes of Johann Valentin Andreae, who published in Germany, in 1619, a book called (in Latin) *A Description of the Republic of Christianopolis*. Andreae's tone is highly moral and religious, and his Utopia is founded on the principle that if men are well-educated, well-disciplined in a just social order, and have their lives rationally organised, they will be happy. He does not propose an end to labour, or technological panaceas, but he does propose that both artisans and women should be educated, making clear also his belief in the virtue of teaching and applying the sciences practically, mathematics for instance. Here is one passage:

Unless you analyze matter by experiment, unless you improve the deficiencies of knowledge by more capable instruments, you are worthless ... Here [in Christianopolis] one may welcome and listen to true and genuine chemistry, free and active, whereas in other places false chemistry steals on one, and imposes on one behind one's back. For true chemistry is accustomed to examine the work, and to make use of experiments. Or, to be brief, here is practical science.

The difficulty is to know exactly what this means.[1]

To return to Hartlib: in the latter part of his life the religious issue was in a sense settled for him first by the Commonwealth and then by the Protectorate – we have no reason to believe that Hartlib was unhappy about the regimes which revolutions in religion established in England. On the other hand we know positively that Hartlib's efforts 'in public services to the

[1] F. E. Held, *Christianopolis* (London, 1916), p. 154.

Commonwealth ... and great services to the Parliament'
were rewarded by grants of money on various occasions, once
as much as £300. So, while continuing to publish on religious
topics, Hartlib devoted more energy in the 1640s and 1650s to
the reform of education and other schemes. To quote John
Dury (another associate, of Scottish origin):

> Mr Hartlib is the solicitor of humane learning for the reformation of
> schooles, and my lot is fallen chiefly in divine matters to promote the
> councils of peace ecclesiastical. As for him, how far he hath advanced his
> work, the things which Mr. Comenius his coadjutor hath put forth (and
> will put forth in due time) for the ways of schooling and pansophical
> learning ... are able to testify for him.[1]

In fact Hartlib was instrumental in publishing, at London
and in English, such works as John Pell's *Idea of Mathematiques*
(1650), Comenius' *Reformation of Schools* (1642), Woodward's
A Light to Grammar (1641), Milton's *Of Education* (1644),
Kinner's *Thoughts on Education* (1648), and so on. It is easy
enough to see why the would-be reformers of society and
religion wished likewise to refurbish the courses of instruction
by which children were formed into citizens. The association
of scholasticism with Catholicism made the old course of logic,
rhetoric and Aristotle peculiarly obnoxious; and in some degree
the reformer's ideas ran toward utilitarianism, as with John
Webster, author of *Examen academiarum* ('Universities on trial'),
who advocated the teaching of chemistry in universities
because of its usefulness in medicine. But this was not, I
believe, a strong note.

I must mention, but not describe in detail, the visit to
England from 1641 to 1642 of the visionary Czech philosopher
and educational reformer, John Amos Comenius, mentioned
in the quotation from John Dury. Comenius was the most
powerful influence on Hartlib, who brought him to England.
He believed in universals – pansophia – as providing the means
to restore a world lost in darkness, war, and error to the way
of truth and light. A universal college would prepare universal
books in a universal language as the basis of a universal
education.

---

[1] See R. H. Syfret, 'The Origins of the Royal Society', *Notes and Records of the
Royal Society*, 5 (1948), 104.

Then [he prophesied] there will be universal Peace over the whole world, hatred and the causes of hatred will be done away and all dissension between men ... Nor will the uncertainties of opinions make any man perplexed when all are taught, not by men who differ from one another in opinions, but by God who is the Truth ... And there will be an age golden in a higher sense than the age of Solomon, then men will return to soundness of mind ... and begin to live indeed, and will devote themselves to a life, rational, spiritual, divine.[1]

Not, be it noted, to a life of material ease, of mechanism, or of power. Comenius' programme, which must be taken as largely Hartlib's also, had to say the least important elements of transcendentalism and mysticism. When Comenius thinks of improving the human lot he is not thinking of two cars in every garage.

We have seen already that Hartlib received his rewards; and he was not wholly lacking in friends or influence. The parliaments that gave him grants were not, it seems, valuing him as technical projector. We can be sure, at any rate, that it was his religious, ethical and moral idealism that commended him to such friends as Milton, the moralist, the excessively pious Lady Ranelagh, and her brother the pious (and later, scientific) Robert Boyle, not to mention John Dury, and these are but a few of those who endorsed Hartlib's ideals.

What then has this to do with science? The answer is a little involved. Clearly, Utopian idealism in England (which is virtually confined to Hartlib's circle) had nothing to do with science directly; it based no expectations on the hope of scientific progress. Only in a very remote way was Hartlib related to the more definite foci of English scientific activity in Gresham College and the universities; besides Robert Boyle, who was for a time much under Hartlib's spell and always respected him, there were Theodore Haak, associated with the origins of the Royal Society, John Pell the mathematician, William Petty and a few more of lesser fame who were both of Hartlib's circle and in the scientific movement – all highly religious and idealistic, with the possible exception of Petty who was a young man on the make. Thus Hartlib might be said to have caused religion, social aspiration, mystical idealism and science to unite in a few people's minds – they

1 Syfret, 'Origins of the Royal Society', p. 113, quoting from Comenius' *Via Lucis*.

are not incompatible – though in my own opinion this has little or nothing to do with the development of science in mid-seventeenth-century England.

If we turn again to the list of Hartlib's publications, especially the later ones, I think we can see the turn Hartlib's activity took, and that it was not towards science – particularly *not* towards those areas of science in which so much progress had been and was to be made, namely the mathematical (astronomy, mechanics, optics) and the medical (anatomy, physiology, microscopy). Instead, Hartlib's name began to be associated (from the late 1640s) with newly invented gadgets and grandiose schemes for making everyone richer. Examples are: William Petty's double-writing instrument and other devices (1648); Richard Weston's *Discourse of Husbandry used in Brabant and Flanders* (1650) – a work of value; Cressy Dymock's *Invention of Engines of Motion* (1651), the usual hopeless mechanical panacea; *The Reformed Husband-man* (1651); John Beale's *Herefordshire Orchards a Pattern for all England* (1657) – the author thought that in England cider should replace wine; and there was much more on beekeeping, silkworms and so on.

I do not propose to take up the question of the influence of these pamphlets on the course of technology in England. I suspect it was slight. This kind of writing was by no means new. Out of the technological literature that had already grown to some size in several languages by this time, one might instance the machine-books (from 1569) puffing all kinds of new mechanical contrivances, and the *Books of Secrets* in the tradition of Cornelius Agrippa, Jerome Cardan and Baptista Porta; the same line had already been pursued in English by Sir Hugh Platt in *The Jewell House of Art and Nature* (1594) and John Bate in *The Mysteryes of Nature and Art* (1631). The only novelty about Hartlib's publications was that he hoped they would illustrate the public utility of his scheme for an 'Office of Address' or universal information bureau, ensuring that the best methods and knowledge were available everywhere in all subjects at all times.

One need hardly elaborate on the point that the encouragement of inventors, projectors and schemers is not the same thing as the encouragement of science, nor indeed as the promotion of the concept (commonly attributed to Francis

Bacon) that scientific knowledge is the road to technical proficiency. I do not believe Hartlib had this concept at all. Certainly there is little sign that he himself gathered this point from Bacon, despite the celebrated tautological opening sentence of the *Novum Organum*:

Man, as the minister and interpreter of Nature, can only do and understand in so far as he has discovered Nature's order, either by thought or by action; he cannot know or do more.

Bacon aroused the interest of Hartlib and Comenius by his plan to win royal patronage for learning, by his proposals for a reformed logic, and by his sketch of a learned college in the *New Atlantis*. Hartlib seems (in the traditional manner) to have visualised invention as the result of 'ingenuity' (like intuition, not a quality born of knowledge), aided by experience of the mysterious powers of Nature. What might be done by winning command of these powers (by whatever means) was virtually limitless; any desideratum, whether the ability to read a person's character from his face, or to convert base metals into gold, or to cure all diseases with a single medicine, or to preserve youth eternally, or to do indefinite amounts of mechanical work with the expenditure of infinitely little energy, was open to a suitably qualified adept. These powers were not to be conquered simply by knowledge of the ordinary sciences of medicine, chemistry, mechanics and so on, because the adept transcended scientific knowledge, as a Prometheus superior to ordinary mortals; *his* powers might run completely counter to the theories and impossibilities propounded by science. Looking at the world from Hartlib's point of view, therefore, it was much less his business to encourage the customary, as we might say, 'academic' sciences (which neither claimed nor aimed to be useful) but to pick out the adepts, the inventors, to have rewards offered to them, to assist in perfecting their secrets, and above all to publicise them. About a century later the Society of Arts was actually founded in London to execute a scheme not unlike Hartlib's, though more rational.

If technological progress or the art of invention is made a kind of mystique, to that extent it is not rational. But I do not believe that it was of great intrinsic importance to Hartlib, though of course this is not to deny his understanding of the utility of making two blades of grass grow where one grew before. Material well-being was only an adjunct to his chief purpose. Let me quote what Dury wrote in explanation of Hartlib's poverty and justification of his merit:

All these objects, but chiefly the civil and ecclesiastical, at this time require so much pains to run up and down, to solicit matters incident and give intelligence by word and writing that it is a thing almost incredible to be believed, if I should report all that I know of it. And to consider but the multitude of things profitable to the public good of every kind, which he doth propose continually to himself and others to be advanced, and which he gathereth together to be freely communicated and imparted to others in matters of schooling, of practical divinity, of ecclesiastical pacification, and of all feats to advance and perfect learning, and also of some things that befall the outward estate of the Churches of God, not in one or two but in all countries, is a thing that would confound any man living, but himself.[1]

Once more, it is clear that Hartlib's circle did not regard his 'attempts for a public good' as including, in any noteworthy way, the promotion of material riches or the attainment of a technological Utopia.

If this is so, then we effectively exclude the possibility that Utopian idealism mediated between science and technology in mid-seventeenth-century England and, indeed, the possibility that Hartlib's seminal group, devoted to learning and the development of the intellect, attached much importance to science on the one hand or to material well-being through technology on the other. Moreover, it means that we cannot use Hartlib's group as a bridge between the nascent scientific movement and the (for the moment) ascendant forces of Puritanism and Revolution. If we could say that Hartlib and his associates were giving a great forward-looking push to science and technical invention for reasons of social idealism, then we could regard them as extreme, but recognised, manifestants of some common Puritan ethos, and so frame an historical interpretation; but if, as I have tried to show, we are *not* justified in conceiving of Hartlib's lifework in this essentially modernist way, this particular link between science (or technology) and victorious Puritanism vanishes.

Hence we must look for alternatives. One aspect of the

[1] G. H. Turnbull, *Hartlib, Dury and Comenius: Gleanings from Hartlib's Papers* (Liverpool, 1947), p. 116.

success of the English scientific movement which is curiously overlooked is that it was the fruit of people who liked science and got on with it. There were enough intellectual problems about the place to rivet anyone's attention. Why are historians looking for an explanation of human interest in science, which is itself a purely intellectual problem, so often reluctant to admit the interest of the intellectual problems provided by science? Wallis, in his recollections of scientific meetings in Commonwealth days, lists a number of these problems for us; the circulation of the blood, and the functions of the lacteal and lymphatic systems; the nature of comets and new stars; the shape of Saturn, sunspots, and the theory of the moon; the improvement of scientific instruments, pneumatics, and mechanics. This list omits problems in Wallis's own subject, mathematics, in chemistry, in optics and in theoretical astronomy of which many Englishmen were also aware. Now the creation of this open frontier of scientific research, rich in controversy and wrangle, was not English; it was, as everyone knows, the creation of continental science, partly through ratiocination, partly through observation and experiment, in which only a few Englishmen, like Harvey and Gilbert, had played a part. The first condition of the scientific achievements among two generations of Englishmen after 1660 was, it is obvious, that their predecessors should pull themselves up to the continental level, that they should learn what the contemporary work in science was and where the arguments lay. The men who brought English thought up to date in one way or another, like the Cavendishes, Sir William Boswell, Theodore Haak, Henry More of Christ's, William Oughtred and John Pell, Sir Kenelm Digby, Thomas Hobbes, Walter Charleton – some Royalist, some Puritan – performed a function without which enthusiasm for science in England would merely have beaten the air. Good work in any subject is impossible unless you know what the significant and possibly soluble problems are, and possess the mental equipment needed for tackling them. If men are interested enough to get this far, then the odds are they will want to have a go at tackling the difficulties themselves.

When continental science had been taken as far as it had (by about 1650) by highly able, professionally skilled and tough-minded men like Galileo, Kepler and Descartes, it was not to be expected that it would be taken further by soft-headed, amateurish or incompetent Englishmen. The fates may have favoured this island at that time, but not as greatly as that. The English scientists of the mid- and later seventeenth century were indeed able, tough-minded, and professional, by no means idealists and dilettantes. They included a number of university teachers like Thomas Willis, John Wallis, John Ray, Henry More and Ralph Cudworth, Isaac Newton, David Gregory, Christopher Wren, and quite a few more; a large group of professional medical men – Richard Lower and John Mayow, William Croone, Nehemiah Grew, Edward Tyson, a host of others; two professional servants of the Royal Society itself, Robert Hooke and Henry Oldenburg, and other serious and active figures, in one way or another, like Robert Boyle and Lord Brouncker, not forgetting John Flamsteed, Astronomer Royal after 1675. These were not just men of great talent; they were men who had trained themselves to be capable of achievement, of participating in the work in mathematics, chemistry, optics, astronomy, physiology and so forth going on all over Europe. The current problems in these various sciences tackled in England were the current problems over all Europe – science was international, critical, competitive in the seventeenth century as it is now. There was no separate little English world of science isolated from the universe and playing the game according to private rules, as though science were a form of cricket. And this pursuit of science by attention to the immediate problems, of which all professionally skilled men were conscious, was little influenced by polemics about the value or otherwise of scientific research, by considerations of the possible utility (in some sense) of this or that discovery or theory, or by outside criteria of any kind. The people who wrote about science in general terms on the whole did little to advance it, and vice versa.

Thus when we list the achievements of English science at this time we find them – not unexpectedly – to be notably abstract, even academic: Willis's study of the brain, Lower's work on respiration, Newton in pure mathematics, mechanics, and optics; Flamsteed's charting of the stars; Ray's cataloguing of British plants, Boyle's work in pneumatics and chemistry.

None of it improved navigation, or medicine, or agriculture. I believe that it was done without thought of such improvement – or that any utilitarian glimmer of motive was at least remote and tangential to the highly personal concern for a problem, something more closely bound up with human egotism and vanity, than with idealism and altruism.

It would be disingenuous to deny that the 'good of mankind' was indeed an object claimed by some of the leaders of English science, and for the Royal Society as a body. Robert Boyle published in 1663 a book entitled *Some Considerations touching the Usefulnesse of Experimental Naturall Philosophy propos'd in familiar Discourses to a Friend, by Way of Invitation to the Study of it*, most of which, Boyle explains, was written long before when he was only about twenty-two years old, and did not altogether represent his maturer views. Boyle's arguments reduce to two:

Firstly, science improves the mind of man: 'The two chief advantages which a real acquaintance with nature brings to our minds are, first, by instructing our understandings and gratifying our curiosities; and next by exciting and cherishing our devotion.' For again, 'there are divers things in nature that do much conduce to the evincing of a Deity, which naturalists either alone discern, or at least discern them better than other men'.[1]

Secondly, science is useful to medicine. The physician, Boyle remarks, 'borrows his principles from the naturalist' that is to say he does, or should, found the principles of his art on the knowledge revealed by the anatomist and physiologist.[2] Further, the insight of the chemist may be useful in accounting for pathological conditions, such as the formation of urinary calculi, as well as in providing remedies for diseases. And generally through scientific knowledge one can extend and strengthen the materia medica.

None of these points was new. As regards medicine, for example, its foundation in science goes back at least to the school of Alexandria, and botany had always been regarded as a branch of materia medica. Boyle was far from suggesting that in such an old-fashioned cramping style the chemist or

---

[1] Robert Boyle, *Works* (ed. T. Birch), (London, 1772), II, pp. 6, 50.
[2] *Ibid.* p. 66.

botanist should only strive to satisfy the physician's need, or that there should only be human dissection and no study of comparative anatomy. His argument is one from the plenitude of knowledge: the more we know, the more we surmount our environment, and specifically the better advised we can be in shaping our medical practice, or prophylactic measures.

Indeed in this same book Boyle alludes to, though he does not elaborate upon, the idea of the empire of man over the lower creation. His scientific skill, he points out, enables man 'to perform such things, as do not only give him a power to master creatures otherwise much stronger than himself, but may enable one man to do such wonders, as another man shall think he cannot sufficiently admire'.[1] Such an empire of the naturalist is to be esteemed over a mere bloody political sovereignty, and is virtual rather than actual since, as Boyle goes on to say, by an ingenious spirit the wonders performed by knowledge are valued rather as proofs of its truth, than as yielding productions, or profits.

Natural knowledge may come still closer to practical affairs: following Bacon, Boyle instances the compass and the discovery of gunpowder as 'secrets of nature' that have transformed human life. So far is true natural knowledge, he says rhetorically, from being barren speculative knowledge that medicine, agriculture and very many trades 'are but corollaries or applications of some few theorems of it'.[2]

The direct argument that science can be useful to trades is further pursued by Boyle in the second, shorter part of the *Usefulness of Natural Philosophy*, written before 1658 but only published in 1671. I will quote Boyle's own summary of the book's purposes:

It may enable gentlemen and scholars to converse with tradesmen, and benefit themselves (and perhaps the tradesmen too) by that conversation ...

It may serve to beget a confederacy, and a union between parts of learning, whose possessors have hitherto kept their respective skills strangers to one another; and by that means may bring great variety of observations and experiments of different kinds into the notice of one man ...

It may contribute to the rescuing natural philosophy from that unhappy imputation of barrenness, which it has so long lain under, and which has been, and still is, so prejudicial to it.[3]

[1] *Ibid.* pp. 14–15. [2] *Ibid.* p. 65. [3] *Ibid.* vol. III, p. 401.

Among Boyle's many examples of the ways in which scientific knowledge can be practically useful there is one which nicely emphasises Boyle's homely and personal notion of this utility. He tells us how, one day, rummaging in a dark neglected cupboard while wearing a new suit of clothes, he had the bad luck to upset and spill on himself the contents of a loosely corked and unlabelled bottle. This would quite have ruined his suit, but judging from the stains that the fluid was an acid, he smelled at the other bottles to see if one might contain an alkali; and 'lighting on a liquor' he says 'which though I knew not what it was I guessed by the stink to abound with volatile salt [ammonia] I bathed the stained parts with it and in a trice restored them to their former colour'. (It was, of course, no small part of Boyle's distinction as a chemist that he appreciated the existence of two classes of acid and alkaline substances, each neutralising the other without respect to individuality.)

In this second book Boyle developed as large claims for the practical utility of science as you will easily find in the seventeenth century. Not that he dwells heavily on all the points; the necessity of geometrical knowledge for surveying, navigation and mechanics, for example. Boyle was a chemical philosopher; it was a great part of his aim in science to show that chemistry was a true part of natural philosophy, and so he insisted mainly on the usefulness of chemical science. But, without enlarging here on the general problem of the utilitarian motive in seventeenth-century science, two other points need to be made. The first is that we must weight Boyle's testimony as that of a young, professed humanitarian enthusiast under Hartlib's influence; other equally distinguished figures of the time put no such testimony on record. Secondly, one must note that the practical good to be derived from science is alleged as only one reason for giving time to it; in the whole work Boyle devoted more argument to the non-materialist reasons. This was quite a normal way of treating the question, as Sir George Clark pointed out long ago.[1] Thirdly, and most of all to the point, Boyle's attitude to the advancement of the crafts through science is (as in the one instance quoted) modest and gradualist. The empire of man over the inferior creation is a

[1] G. N. Clark, *Science and Social Welfare in the Age of Newton* (Oxford, 1937).

proper and desirable object, and it may be enhanced by scientific knowledge, but Boyle is far from suggesting that any sweeping, miraculous benefits can follow, or that society will be enormously transformed for the better by increased technical skill alone. He was far too moral and Christian a man to hold such an opinion, and therefore he disclosed no prospect of a technological Utopia.

A man markedly influenced by both Samuel Hartlib and Robert Boyle was Henry Oldenburg, yet another German *émigré*, who was Secretary of the Royal Society from 1662 until his death in 1677. Like Hartlib, Oldenburg was a man with a conventional learned background having an emphasis on theology. In the mid 1650s signs appear in his correspondence of the modernist intellectual influences to which he had been subjected since his arrival in London. First in order of time and logic he expresses frequent criticism of conventional philosophy and theology. In Oxford, he writes:

I seem to see some few men who bend their minds to solid studies rather than to others, and, disgusted with scholastic theology and nominalist philosophy, have begun to embrace both Nature and truth.[1]

And in another place he condemns the 'professional type of scholar ... who makes return for the food he receives by nothing but foolish and irritating braying'. By contrast, those are true sons of learning who try to unfold Nature's innermost secrets. Unfortunately, though the conventional image of the quibbling, futile academic pedant is clear enough, one does not know precisely what such a man as Oldenburg set on the other side at this time: probably the members of the Oxford scientific group, including such men as Wilkins, Wallis, Boyle himself, Wren, Willis and so on. There is no note of practical utility here. In the later 1650s, however, some of Hartlib's interest in inventions and new devices was infused into Oldenburg, and by the time the Royal Society is founded he sees its objects as combining elements both of philosophical reform and utility to the life of man.

So he writes, early in 1663:

It is our business in the first place to scrutinize Nature and to investigate its activity and powers by means of observations and experiments; and

[1] A. Rupert Hall & Marie Boas Hall, *The Correspondence of Henry Oldenburg* (Madison & Milwaukee, 1965) vol. I, p. 95.

then in course of time to hammer out a more solid philosophy and more ample amenities of civilization (*philosophiam solidorem et ampliora vitae civilis commoda*).[1]

Only a few weeks later in another letter he puts the same point thus:

> It is now our business, having already established under royal favour this assembly of philosophers who cultivate the world of arts and sciences by means of observation and experiment, and who advance them in order to safeguard human life and make it more pleasant, to attract to the same purpose men from all parts of the world ... (etc.)[2]

Somewhat the same formula recurs over the years. The following quotation from a letter of late 1668 is more or less picked at random:

> I was very much pleased to find your skill employed for the advancement of the knowledge of Nature, and the earnest desire to serve the Royal Society by contributing what you can to the carrying on of their design, which is nothing else but the study of Nature by observations and experiments accurately and faithfully made, thereby to glorify the God of Nature and to benefit mankind by useful discoveries.[3]

Hence Oldenburg's vision of the intellectual Utopia of the future is a state of knowledge in which a complete and reliable history of Nature in all her aspects has been compiled, and serves in turn as the basis for a no less complete philosophy of Nature or body of theoretical skill, which will satisfy all men's intellectual problems, fill them with a duly informed admiration for the Creator, and minister to their physical needs, particularly as regards medicine.

This is some of the evidence. On consideration, it seems that these English idealists and reformers suffered severely from the narrowness of the antithesis to which their tradition and their inexperience drew them – the antithesis between empty verbalising on the one hand, and practical or religious usefulness on the other. There is a good deal of knowledge in between, as everyone could recognise at times, for example when Oldenburg wrote to Thomas Hobbes to ask his opinion of the usefulness of mathematics. The question was not asked, he said, 'for any use of trade, but of enriching and entertaining the mind, both with the theory and the particular knowledge

---

[1] *Ibid.* vol. II, p. 14.   [2] *Ibid.* vol. II, p. 27.   [3] *Ibid.* vol. V, p. 95.

of the use of that theory ... seeing this demonstrative knowledge stayeth and satisfieth the mind as much as food doth an
empty stomach' and thus even has, he goes on, a wider social
value.[1] But, when looking merely for a contrast to the dis-
putatious emptiness of scholasticism (as the new philosophers
saw it) they were apt to fail to distinguish the many applications
of the word *useful*.

It is perhaps worth pointing out too that these same seventeenth-century Englishmen confused two avenues of progress.
One course was that of scientific development proper, taken
by the professionally competent men mentioned above,
whether experimentalists or mathematicians. This was the
important avenue, beyond dispute. It did not lead *only* to
the conveniences of human life, as we have seen. The other
route was that of the inventors and adepts, the discoverers
of secrets from the philosopher's stone to a cure for boils.
Of its very nature this avenue was intensely practical; its
exponents promised health, long life, and rich profits, and
certainly aimed to reap profits themselves. In my opinion
the purveyors of secrets from Drebbel to Becher contributed
little to the scientific revolution, though the seductive lure of
secrets – arcana – touched some of its greatest figures, including
Boyle and Leibniz. Hartlib devoted endless trouble to pursuing
secrets all over Europe – lamps, clocks, explosives, agricultural
routines, perpetual motion devices, medical remedies and so
on. In the context of his time it was easy to conflate the pursuit
of scientific learning (carrying the incidental hope of ultimate
utility) with the pursuit of secrets or practical arcana, fusing
them into a single search for both knowledge and power;
it was the more easy because the methods of scientific investigation were by no means sharply divorced, as yet, from the
esoteric or Hermetic way that was supposed to lead to the
profoundest arcana. But, as historians, we must and should
make this distinction, which is not one introduced by ourselves
since the seventeenth century was, in principle, aware of it
too.

What of the idealist element that is peculiarly associated
with Utopian schemes, or visions? I do not think it ran counter
to the traditional estimation of the dignity of learning, especially

[1] *Ibid.* vol. I, p. 75.

of knowledge of Nature for its own sake, because Utopists did
not deny the value of all knowledge that is true, and not a
mere verbal technique. In the mid-seventeenth century
English idealists saw Utopia as attainable by bringing a
community of men to the true religion, by bringing out the
moral side of human nature, by creating optimal social
conditions and enacting just laws, and finally by making it
possible for men to attain real knowledge which could be
devoted to the common good. Technical excellence was not
seen as a sufficient or even a necessary condition for an ideal
society, and science was certainly not esteemed merely as a
key to technical excellence.

Even Bacon in the *New Atlantis* takes the same view, though
far more than any later writer he stressed the scientific and
technical wonders to be found in Salomon's House, the
description of which was apparently his chief motive for
composing this fiction. It is unnecessary for me to describe
Bacon's vision of what a theoretical and practical research
institute might be like; even for its own time it was pretty
absurd, and though the conception had some influence
Bacon's specification did not, I think. Discovery and invention
are united in Salomon's House, and it is the business of the
Fathers of the House to disseminate all that is useful: 'The
end of our foundation is the knowledge of causes and secret
motions of things; and the enlarging of the bounds of human
Empire to the effecting of all things possible'. Bacon's
examples – the high towers and deep caves, the experimental
gardens and menageries, the pharmaceutical laboratories and
mechanical workshops, and so on – are well enough known.
What perhaps is easy to overlook is that he does not ascribe
the happiness of Bensalem to Salomon's House: rather he
ascribes happiness to its isolation from impure communities,
its pristine Christianity and simple morality, its wise unchanging
laws and ethical code. As the Traveller is told, 'there is nothing
amongst mortal men more fair and admirable than the chaste
minds of this people'.

Only within such a context of virtue were the inhabitants
of Bensalem to be entrusted with the knowledge and power
attributed to their Salomon's House. Neither Bacon, nor
Hartlib, nor Boyle would have imagined that happiness or

social justice could result from command of means alone, without religion and virtue to dictate the ends. If a philosopher contemplated a society without evil, then (without adding much to incredulity) he might contemplate its also being free from ignorance, pain and toil. But he would not, it seems to me, ever have supposed that knowledge or power could be substituted for virtue, or that a non-virtuous, irreligious society could be ideal.

3

WHO UNBOUND PROMETHEUS? SCIENCE AND TECHNICAL CHANGE, 1600–1800[1]

by Peter Mathias

I

An economic historian is interested in science not for its own sake (which for an historian of science is doubtless the only academically respectable way of looking at it) but for his own utilitarian purposes. He asks the questions: how was science related to technology at this time? how far did scientific change influence the process of technological change? to what extent was the Industrial Revolution associated with scientific advance? Taking the very long view from medieval times to the present day is to see a dramatic change in these relationships. Broadly we may postulate the earlier position as a context where empirical discoveries and the development of industrial processes in such industries as metals, textiles, brewing, dyeing took place and advanced without being directly consequential upon knowledge of fundamental scientific relationships in the materials concerned. The chemistry of what happened inside a blast furnace was not known until the mid-decades of the nineteenth century. The secrets of fermentation were first revealed by Pasteur. There might be close links between science and technology in other ways, but this was nonetheless a world very different from our own where industrial advance becomes more directly consequential upon the advancing frontier of scientific and technological knowledge, with a developing institutional relationship between science and industry to consolidate the connection.

For the pivotal period of the seventeenth and eighteenth

---

[1] An early version of this article appeared in the *Yorkshire Bulletin of Economic and Social Research*, XXI (1) (1969).

centuries, however, which saw dramatic advances in both scientific knowledge and industrial techniques, varying answers have been offered to these questions by economic historians and scholars generalising about the relationships from the side of science. Professor A. R. Hall summed up for the earlier period 1660–1760 'we have not much reason to believe that in the early stages, at any rate, learning or literacy had anything to do with it [technological change]; on the contrary, it seems likely that virtually all the techniques of civilisation up to a couple of hundred years ago were the work of men as uneducated as they were anonymous.'[1] Sir Eric Ashby concludes for the period 1760–1860: 'There were a few 'cultivators of science' (as they were called) engaged in research, but their work was not regarded as having much bearing on education and still less on technology. There was practically no exchange of ideas between the scientists and the designers of industrial processes.'[2] Professor Landes is equally firm in this opinion to as late as 1850.[3] A. P. Usher is in the same tradition.[4]

Equally forthright assertions crowd the other side of the stage. 'The stream of English scientific thought', wrote Professor Ashton, 'was one of the main tributaries of the Industrial Revolution ... The names of engineers, ironmasters, industrial chemists, and instrument makers on the list of Fellows of the Royal Society show how close were the relations between science and practice at this time.'[5] Professor Rostow, considering the whole sweep of economic change in Western Europe, gives the two essential features of postmedieval Europe as 'the discovery and re-discovery of regions beyond Western Europe, and the initially slow but then accelerating development of modern scientific knowledge and attitudes'.[6] When considering the essential propensities for

[1] A. R. Hall, *The Historical Relations of Science and Technology* (inaugural lecture) (London, 1963); J. D. Bernal, *Science in History* (London, 1954), pp. 345–6, 352, 354–5, 365–6, 370, argues in a similar vein.

[2] Sir E. Ashby, *Technology and the Academics* (London, 1958), pp. 50–1.

[3] D. Landes in *Cambridge Economic History of Europe*, vol. VI, pt. 1 (Cambridge, 1965), pp. 333, 343, 550–1; also *The Unbound Prometheus* (Cambridge, 1969), pp. 104, 113–14, 323.

[4] A. P. Usher, *A History of Mechanical Invention* (Boston, 1954 ed.) contains very little reference to the role of science in this period.

[5] T. S. Ashton, *The Industrial Revolution* (London, 1948), pp. 15–16.

[6] W. W. Rostow, *The Stages of Economic Growth* (Cambridge, 1960), p. 31.

economic growth (relationships that he does not specifically
limit in time or place) the first two on his list are: 'the
propensity to develop fundamental science and to apply
science to economic ends'.[1] For the English case Musson and
Robinson have recently sought to demonstrate how extensive
the linkages were between innovation and science, between
scientists and entrepreneurs.[2] They see this co-operation
assisting England to 'retain that scientific lead over the continent upon which she established her industrial supremacy'.[3]
The Lunar Society, now documented at great length,
has been called 'a pilot project or advance guard of
the Industrial Revolution' on the argument that 'strong
currents of scientific research underlie critical parts of this
movement'.[4]

Many more such summary assertions could be deployed
on either side. It seems likely that, as historians explore more
systematically and in more local detail the development of
different branches of the chemical industry and other
industrial processes involving chemistry (following up the
seminal work on the Chemical Revolution by A. and A. N.
Clow, published in 1952); as they find out more about the
various local societies of gentlemen meeting in small towns
up and down the country in the eighteenth century on the
lines of the Lunar Society of Birmingham, the balance will
tip heavily towards the positive equation. This theme is
captured in the remark: 'science is the mother of invention;
finance is its father'.[5]

The question, therefore, invites discussion. The arguments,
however, should be prefaced with one or two comments.
Without the assumption that a simple, linear, cause-and-effect

[1] W. W. Rostow, *The Process of Economic Growth* (New York, 1952), p. 23.
[2] A. E. Musson and E. Robinson, 'Science and Industry in the late 18th Century',
    Economic History Review, XIII (1960), 222–4; *Science and Technology in the Indus-
    trial Revolution* (Manchester, 1969).
[3] E. Robinson, 'The Lunar Society and the Improvement of Scientific Instruments
    II', *Annals of Science*, XIII (1957).
[4] R. E. Schofield, *The Lunar Society of Birmingham* (Oxford, 1963), pp. 437, 410.
    The argument is summed up on pp. 436–40. See also the special issue of the
    University of Birmingham Historical Journal, XI, no. 1 (1967), devoted to the Lunar
    Society, particularly the articles by E. Robinson, M. J. Wise and R. E.
    Schofield; E. Robinson, 'The Lunar Society Its Membership and Organisation',
    Transactions of the Newcomen Society, XXXV (1962–3).
[5] T. H. Marshall, *James Watt* (London, 1925), p. 84.

relationship exists between phenomena like scientific knowledge and innovations in technique, multi-dimensional historical developments such as the Renaissance or the French Revolution or the Fall of the Roman Empire or the Industrial Revolution, cease to be analysable in terms of single-cause, single-variable phenomena. In the last analysis, quantification of contributory causes of them is impossible, given the intractable nature of the evidence and the subtlety of the inter-relationships, direct and indirect, involved. Therefore, no intellectually satisfying proof becomes possible that one answer is demonstrably 'correct' in a scientifically provable way. Quantification does not offer any obvious solution either. One might hope that, taking a defined population of innovations, it would be possible to determine the percentage which depended upon scientific knowledge, or to allocate degrees of such dependence upon some quantified scale. But establishing the criteria of such a scale would be subjective enough, while yet greater discretion would remain in allocating most innovations to the different boxes. Moreover innovations form a most heterogeneous collection, differing very greatly in relative importance. Bringing qualitative considerations into the argument would imply further discretionary allocation of innovations into a scale of importance so that the degree of dependence of innovations upon scientific knowledge could be construed against some norm of economic significance. Were the scientifically-orientated innovations in the 'population' more, or less, important than their arithmetical proportion suggests?

The question of the *strategic* importance of innovations raises a further issue. For example, despite the percentage of total technical change subject to the linkage with science being small, a strategic blockage on a narrow front at the frontier of technical possibilities might hold up innovation in a wider span behind it. One strategic science-linked innovation could make possible a large number of empirically-based innovations which were, to a degree, dependent upon that initial advance, and vice versa. Moreover, it is impossible to demonstrate the potential quantitative importance of this by being able to indicate what would have happened if an absolute blockage at the frontier had occurred without substitute arrangements bypassing the obstruction. Perhaps

E   57

detailed analysis can be applied in the micro-study of particular innovations (carefully chosen), but it is difficult to see how a quantified assessment can be made for the wide sweep of innovations under discussion here. History is a depressingly inexact science as economists – let alone natural scientists – discover to their frustration.

Conclusions in this field are also much influenced by methodological or definitional problems. Controversies on such general themes characteristically sink under the weight of semantic disagreement and pleas for more systematic research. What do we include in (or exclude from) the concept 'innovation'? Were the activities of these seventeenth- and eighteenth-century people, properly speaking 'scientific'? Was it *real* science, identified by some later, designated, objective norm – in the 'Baconian' mechanistic tradition – or was it bogus, mistaken, irrational – and following a magical, alchemical or Hermetical tradition?[1] How much, for example, can one claim for Jethro Tull, eagerly pursuing 'scientific' technique in agriculture on the assumption that air was the greatest of all manures and that the fertility of soil consequently varied in direct correlation with the amount of ploughing and pulverising that it received, to the exclusion of all else. Bogus science, quasi science, mistaken science, amateur science which was so very prominent in the seventeenth and eighteenth centuries, particularly in the field of chemistry (where the direct linkage between science and industry are probably most diffused) does raise interesting issues. Does one judge these practitioners by their intentions, their motivations or by their results, however mistaken their assumptions, looked at *ex post facto* with hindsight.

Arguments about distinctions between 'pure' and 'applied' science relate to these controversies, for the seventeenth and eighteenth centuries no less than the nineteenth and twentieth.[2]

This paper will first explore the positive case and then

---

[1] P. Rattansi, 'The Social Interpretation of Science in the Seventeenth Century', above, pp. 1–32.

[2] R. K. Merton, 'Science, Technology and Society in Seventeenth Century England', *Osiris*, IV (1938); A. R. Hall, 'Merton revisited: Science and Society in the Seventeenth Century', *History of Science*, II (1963); C. C. Gillespie, 'The Natural History of Industry', *Isis*, XLVIII (1957).

consider its qualifications.[1] The key question to be answered
is not what examples can be found of links between science and
industry in the period but rather how important relative to
other sources of impetus was scientific knowledge to industrial
progress? Can it be judged 'an engine of growth' for innovation,
or a pre-condition? In short, how extensive were the linkages,
how strategic, how direct?

II

If economic history is written from the evidence of intention,
of aspiration and endeavour, rather than the evidence of
results (which is often less accessible) then these connections
appear very intimate indeed. In the first place, a very large
number of persons – scientists, industrialists, publicists, and
government servants – said loudly in the seventeenth century
and have gone on saying ever since then, even more loudly,
that the linkage was important and ought to be encouraged.
For most of the 'professional' scientists of the Restoration
the improvement of techniques in the material world, science
in the service of a technological Utopia, was a subordinate
quest, a relatively low priority. But, even so, many such as
Robert Boyle were active on both sides of the watershed
between searching for knowledge and applying knowledge to
practice, and certainly acknowledged that *one* of the roles of
science was to help where it could. Boyle's *Usefulness of Natural
Philosophy* (1664) was a systematic survey of the methods then
used in industry and of the ways in which science was improving
them and would continue to do so. 'These [mechanical] arts',
he wrote, 'ought to be looked upon as really belonging to the

---

[1] An equivalent, and connected debate, which will not be considered here, is
in progress over these relationships, and that of religion in the seventeenth
century. See H. F. Kearney, *Origins of the Scientific Revolution* (London, 1964);
C. Hill, *The Intellectual Origins of the English Revolution* (Oxford, 1965); C. Hill,
H. F. Kearney, and T. K. Rabb in *Past and Present*, XXVIII, 81; XXIX, 88; XXXI,
104, 111; XXXII, 110. The thesis was formulated by R. K. Merton, 'Science,
Society and Technology in Seventeenth Century England', *Osiris* (1938).
See also S. F. Mason, 'The Scientific Revolution and the Protestant Revolution', *Annals of Science*, IX (1953); D. S. Kemsley, 'Religious Influences in
the Rise of Modern Science', *Annals of Science*, XXIV (1968). This, in turn, is
an extension of the much older debate about the links between protestantism and
capitalism, from Max Weber.

history of nature in its full and due extent.'[1] 'There is much real benefit to be learned [from mathematical or philosophical inquiries?]', wrote Dr J. Wilkins in 1648, 'particularly for such gentlemen as employ their estates in those chargeable adventures of Drayning, Mines, Cole-pits, etc. . . . And also for such *common artificers* as are well skilled in the *practise* of the arts.'[2] Boyle was himself active particularly in investigating the techniques of mining, assaying and agriculture. In evidence of intention, if not of result, John Richardson changed the title of his book on *Philosophical Principles of the Art of Brewing*, much taken up by the largest brewers in London, to *Philosophical Principles of the Science of Brewing*.[3] R. Shannon's more empirically titled work *Practical Treatise on Brewing* was primarily a plea that brewers and distillers should profit from contact with 'men of reflection acquainted with first principles who have more methodically considered the subject'. 'Chemistry', he remarked, 'is as much the basis of arts and manufactures, as mathematics is the fundamental principle of mechanics.'[4] They were echoing a traditional sentiment which continued to reverberate until scientific discoveries with major implications for technology in the industry really were made by Pasteur and others in the mid-nineteenth century.

Two eminent Victorians out of many, may be quoted to show the canon during the nineteenth century. Charles Babbage, writing *On the Economy of Machinery and Manufactures* (1835) concluded: 'it is impossible not to perceive that the arts and manufactures of the country are intimately connected with the progress of the severer sciences; and that, as we advance in the career of improvement, every step requires, for its success, that this connexion should be rendered more intimate'.[5] Dr Lyon Playfair, the forward-looking Scot who helped to organise the Great Exhibition of 1851 wrote, with justly famous perception: 'Raw material, formerly our capital

---

1 Cf. A. R. Hall, *Ballistics in the Seventeenth Century* (Cambridge, 1952), p. 3; also G. N. Clark, *Science and Social Welfare in the Age of Newton* (Oxford, 1937), p. 14.

2 J. Wilkins, *Mathematical Magick* ... (London, 1649), p. vi.

3 J. Richardson, *Philosophical Principles of the Art of Brewing* (Hull, 1788); *Philosophical Principles of the Science of Brewing* (Hull, 1798).

4 R. Shannon, *Practical Treatise on Brewing* (1804), pp. 48–9.

5 C. Babbage, *On the Economy of Manufactures* (London, 1835), p. 379, para. 453.

advantage over other nations, is gradually being equalised in price, and made available to all by improvements in locomotion, and Industry must in future be supported, not by a competition of local advantages, but by a competition of intellects.'[1] The assertion of the linkage has formed a continuum; and still does.

Apart from such aspirations look also at what endeavours actually took place. The state actively sought to press scientists into utilitarian endeavour. A long list of instances can be drawn up. Typical examples are ballistics and navigation (improvements in cartography, scientific instruments, astronomy, mathematical tables, accurate time-keeping lay behind this). Much medical experimentation went on sponsored by the Admiralty, facing particular problems of maintaining efficiency in fleets, long on foreign station, from scurvy and other diseases. Standardisation in production, in dockyards, of interchangeable parts, exact measurement techniques, were much encouraged. Industrial and scientific skills likely to be useful in war received particular attention. More widely, national rivalries became important in the seventeenth century for stimulating inventions in many industries where there was most technical progress – export industries, sugar refining, distilling, glass blowing, silk, tobacco, book printing, paper making and others.[2]

The Royal Society in England, of 1662, as the French *Académie* of 1666, personified such state patronage (although in England with virtually no public resources) for utilitarian ends, an intention explicitly stated in its first charter. The draft preamble of the statutes of the Royal Society ran: 'The business of the Royal Society is: to improve the knowledge of natural things, and all useful arts, Manufactures, Mechanic practices, Engynes and Inventions by experiment.'[3] Nothing could be more explicit. Its first historian stressed this need to focus the work of scientists upon technology; in the words

---

[1] Lyon Playfair, *Lectures on the Results of the Great Exhibition of 1851* (London, 1852). Royal Commissions joined the chorus in 1864 with the publication of the Taunton Commission report on technical and scientific education. Mark Pattison made the same plea in *Suggestions on Academical Organisation . . .* (Edinburgh, 1868).

[2] Clark, *Science and Social Welfare*, pp. 51ff.

[3] See also M. Ornstein, *The role of Scientific Societies in the 17th Century* (Chicago, 1928), pp. 108–9. For details of the utilitarian aims of the French *Académie des Sciences* see ch. 5.

of Thomas Sprat in 1667 its work was intended 'for the use of cities and not for the retirements of Schools'.[1] Pepys urged its members to 'principally aim at such experiments or observations as might prove of great and immediate use', and had the record searched for helps to navigation. The King, petitioned by 'projectors' with secret weapons to save an industry or confound the French, referred such proposals to the Society for vetting and report. Members divided themselves into special committees for this purpose. The *Philosophical Transactions* in the seventeenth century exemplify the common concern; experiments and reports intended to have practical applications, to agriculture as well as industry, had as much space or more devoted to them as any other. This surely, is the breeding ground for innovation. The spark then jumps from the metropolitan scene of the Royal Society in its early days to the many provincial societies linking amateur scientists with gentlemen-manufacturers in the Lunar Society of Birmingham and very many others of lesser renown. Relatively obscure towns like Spalding, Northampton, Peterborough and Maidstone for example, boasted such gatherings. Almost thirty are known to have existed.[2]

William Shipley called the Northampton Philosophical Society specifically a 'Royal Society in Miniature' – 'a Society of Gentlemen that are much addicted to all manner of natural knowledge'.[3] Most of these local societies had the specific aim of popularising science and using scientific knowledge for practical ends in the improvement of practical skills in industry and agriculture – as with the national institutions of the Society of Arts (1754) founded by William Shipley and the Royal Institution (1799), founded by Count Rumford, both of whom were passionate advocates of the application of science.

---

[1] T. Sprat, *History of the Royal Society* (London, 1667). See also J. G. Crowther, *The Social Relations of Science* (1967 ed.), pp. 274–87; C. R. Weld, *A History of the Royal Society* ... (London, 1848), vol. I, pp. 146ff; vol. IV, section V; M. Purver, *The Royal Society: Concept and Creation* (London, 1967).

[2] D. McKie, 'Scientific Societies to the end of the 18th Century' in A. Ferguson ed. *Natural Philosophy Through the 18th Century* (1948); E. Robinson, 'The Derby Philosophical Society', *Annals of Science*, IX (1953); R. E. Schofield, *The Lunar Society* (Oxford, 1963); D. Hudson and K. W. Luckhurst, *The Royal Society of Arts* (London, 1954).

[3] D. G. C. Allan, *William Shipley* (London, 1968), p. 169.

Next look at a growing list of examples of innovations which sprang, or appeared to spring, from this fertile soil of scientific discourse and social nexus between the men of science and industry. Steam-power above all; but also the adolescent chemical industry with chlorine-bleaching, sulphuric-acid production, soda making, coal distillation.[1] James Watt, Dr John Roebuck, Josiah Wedgwood, Lord Dundonald, George and Charles Macintosh are the most well-known individuals who personify these connections. The *extent* of interest in 'amateur science' coupled with the extent of endeavour in relating science to industry is remarkable, and in this England is certainly unique in Europe. The important research of Musson and Robinson has placed all economic historians in their debt by revealing how extensive these interests were – almost, one might say, a 'sub-culture' of interest in science, faith in the possibilities of applying science, and enthusiastic advocacy.

In fact, mathematics may well have played a wider role in these relationships than science until the end of the eighteenth century. Navigation techniques and improvements at sea (not alone sponsored by the navy), land surveying techniques for estates, accountancy for business, assaying, architectural drawing, spectacle making are examples of practical skills that gained and were seen to gain, from mathematical knowledge. The Nonconformist and Quaker groups gave a prominent place to modern studies, particularly mathematics, that had a greater presence in new educational movements than science.[2] The observations of a distinguished user of the new mathematical knowledge for practical purposes underline this truth:

We are sure of finding a Ship's place at Sea to a Degree and a half and generally to less than half a Degree, [wrote Captain James Cook]. Such are the improvements Navigation has received from the Astronomers of the Age by the Valuable Table they have communicated to the Publick under the direction of the Board of Longitude ... [By] these Tables the Calculations are rendered short beyond conception and easy to the

---

[1] A long bibliography is contained in A. E. Musson and E. Robinson, *Science and Technology in the Industrial Revolution* (Manchester, 1969).

[2] S. Pollard, *The Genesis of Modern Management* (London, 1965), ch. 4; J. D. Bernal, *Science in History* (London, 1954) p. 346; N. Hans, *New Trends in Education in the Eighteenth Century* (London, 1951). A Mathematical Society was established in Spitalfields in 1717, and another at Manchester in 1718 (T. Kelly, *G. Birkbeck – Pioneer of Adult Education* (Liverpool, 1957) p. 66).

meanest capacity and can never be enough recommended to the Attention
of all Sea Officers ... Much credit is also due to the Mathematical
Instrument Makers for the improvements and accuracy with which their
instruments are made for without good instruments the Tables would lose
part of their use.[1]

The utility of such mathematical expertise, coupled with
precision measurement by new instruments, for a trading,
industrial, seafaring nation was sufficient for it to become
institutionalised in schools on a fairly wide scale in eighteenth-
century England. Rather than enlarge the catalogue of
instances, however, let us now move to looking at some of the
problems – acknowledging that a long list of such individual
instances exists. It is the nature of the connections between
science and technical change, no less than the extent of the
association between them which is in question.

III

The first complication is, perhaps, not a fundamental one
within the European scene, although it raises important
questions when relating science to innovation within a single
country; or perhaps even more fundamentally when one
compares scientific knowledge and its relation to technique
(the general level of diffused technique rather than individual
instances of 'best practice' technology) in Europe and beyond –
say in China. The point is, simply, that we are much concerned
with differences between national performances in industrial
growth and innovation, in striving to explain the fact that the
British economy advanced more extensively than others in
this way, and became *relatively* so much more forward in
adopting new techniques and developing new industries in
1750–1850 than other economies. This is particularly true of
the general level of technique, productivity and output
characterising growth industries (textiles, metal production,
metal-using techniques, machine tools, machine making,
particularly power engineering, chemicals, pottery, glass).

Scientific knowledge does not show, at all, the same concentration within Britain, particularly in the case of chemistry

---

[1] *Journals of Capt. James Cook (1768–1779)* ed. A. Grenfell Price (New York,
Heritage Press, n.d.) pp. 112–13 (for 14 January 1773).

where the linkage between scientific knowledge and industrial innovation was probably most intimate. The advance of scientific knowledge was a European phenomenon. There was, in France, much greater state patronage for science through the *Académie des Sciences*, by military sponsorship, and direct industrial sponsorship, as with the research department attached to the Sèvres porcelain factory working on glazes, enamels and paints. Provincial academies also flourished in the main regional cities.[1] In the *Description des Arts et Métiers* of Réamur 1761 one had a more elaborate schema published than any known in Britain. On balance, more systematic work was carried out in technology by scientists in France than on this side of the Channel. Countries innocent of industrialisation (but with pressing military needs) also established equivalent academies, with state patronage for the useful arts – especially arts useful for military success – supported by much private interest. Sweden, Russia, Prussia and Italy are examples.[2] A Royal Irish Academy also flourished. The 'Dublin Society for Improving Husbandry, Manufactures and other Useful Arts' was the first of the 'popularising' associations, established in 1731. The Welsh Society of Cymmrodorion followed in 1751. One of the earlier of the agricultural improvement societies was that of Brecknockshire, founded in 1753.[3] Evidence of motivation the institutionalising of practical science in these societies clearly was; but it may well have come, in such instances, where the need was greatest, rather than where the links were closest. It should also be said that the English societies flourished with very tiny material resources indeed, being amateur and self-financing. The very small cash premiums or medals they offered as inducements to inventors cannot be seen as 'research and development' costs in the modern sense of capital investment in innovation. The fact that endeavour was stimulated by the chance of winning a medal offered by such a private society or

---

[1] F. A. Yates, *The French Academies of the 16th Century* (London, 1911); H. Brown, *Scientific Organisations in 17th Century France* (New York, 1934).

[2] R. Hahn, 'The application of Science to Society: the Societies of Arts', *Studies on Voltaire and the Eighteenth Century*, XXIV–XXVII (Geneva, 1963), 829–36. This article lists a dozen such societies in different countries.

[3] H. F. Berry, *A History of the Royal Dublin Society* (London, 1915); Allan, *William Shipley*, p. 61.

appearing in its transactions, says much for the prestige attached to science and to the quest for 'improvement' in practical matters. But, clearly these investments and endeavours could be made on a scale more extensive absolutely than England (in the case of France) and on a scale relatively greater (judged against the resources of the country) without much of a 'spin off' giving a boost to industrial growth.

The French record of scientific growth and invention in the eighteenth century was a formidable one.[1] Berthollet first revealed to the world the bleaching possibilities of chlorine, first isolated as a gas in 1774 by a Swedish chemist Scheele, which was followed by energetic efforts to promote its manufacture in France. A similar sequence followed with Leblanc making soda from salt and sulphuric acid.[2] Very sophisticated work was done in the production of dyestuffs in France; with varnishes, enamels and many other techniques and materials. Yet the difference in the rate of industrial growth based on these advances in chemistry between France and Britain in the period 1780 and 1850 was remarkable. Almost all the theoretical work on structures, stresses and the mechanics of design in civil engineering was French. This did not appear to have much relationship to the speed of development, or even innovations in these fields, as far as economic progress was concerned. The same was true of power engineering and hydrodynamics.[3] The record of development and implementation was also significantly different from the record of invention.

The wider question, not to be pursued here, is even more interesting. The sophisticated scientific mechanical knowledge in China produced even less impetus to the general levels of industrial technique representative of that vast region, or to industrial growth. It remained more sealed up in a small

---

[1] See, in illustration, S. T. McCloy, *French Inventions of the Eighteenth Century* (Lexington, Ky, 1952) and *Government Assistance in Eighteenth Century France* (Durham, N.C. 1946).

[2] C. C. Gillespie, 'The Discovery of the Leblanc Process', *Isis*, XLVIII (1957).

[3] D. S. L. Cardwell, 'Power Technologies and the Advancement of Science, 1700–1825', *Technology and Culture* (1965) vol. VI; 'Some Factors in the Early Development of the Concept of Power, Work and Energy', *British Journal for the History of Science*, III (1966–7); R. Hahn, *L'hydrodynamique au XVIIIᵉ siècle* (Paris, 1965); D. Landes, *Cambridge Economic History of Europe* (Cambridge, 1965), vol. VI, p. 333.

Who unbound Prometheus?

enclave of scholars, civil servants, and isolated groups under
noble and royal patronage than in – say – St Petersburg. By
itself, therefore, it becomes difficult to argue that a flow of
new scientific knowledge and applied science is a key variable;
it may be a pre-condition for advance, but it does not necessarily
give the operational impetus.

Secondly, the problem of time lags between knowledge and
action raises awkward problems for the 'positive' one-to-one
equation in its simple form. The economic historian is more
interested in innovation and the diffusion of innovations than
in invention for its own sake. Putting inventions to productive
use involves all the costs and problems of translation from
laboratory technique into industrial production, from the
largely non-commercial context of the pursuit of knowledge to
profitability as a condition of existence. One is not even very
interested in isolated examples of new industrial techniques
but rather in their diffusion to the point when innovations begin
to affect general levels of output, costs, productivity in an
industry; when their adoption is on a sufficient scale to affect
the performance of the industry significantly. To mention a
few of these astonishing time lags. The screw-cutting lathe,
foundation of the precision engineering skills which made an
efficient machine-making industry possible, was clearly documented by Leonardo da Vinci in the *Note-Books*, laid out
again in the section on watch-making tools in the *Description
des Arts et Métiers* in mid-eighteenth-century France and
developed, spontaneously, again by Maudslay, to become –
from that innovation – the basis of a progeny of machine tools.
Sir T. Lombe's silk throwing machine, which was used for the
first time in a factory in England in 1709, had been used and
known in Italy since 1607 – with an accurate engraving in a
book on the open shelves of the Bodleian Library by 1620.[1]
The same is true of gearing and the design of gear wheels,
bridge design, pumps, Archimedean screws, the 'pound' lock,
mass production needle-grinding machines and a host of
others (all to be found in Leonardo's work).[2] In certain
respects, steam power is another example. The pound lock –
being the basic technology of a dry dock – was known in

[1] Quoted Clark, *Science and Social Welfare*.
[2] I. B. Hart, *The World of Leonardo da Vinci* (London, 1961).

67

Dutch shipyards in the fifteenth century, perhaps much earlier, and appeared in England in the sixteenth century. But a still-water canal system of which this is the only important piece of technology was an eighteenth-century phenomenon in Britain.[1] Equally dramatic time lags exist in the opposite direction – between empirical improvements in technique and the beginning of scientific interest in explaining them.[2]

Bound up with this problem of time lags between knowledge and invention, invention and adoption, adoption and diffusion are correlated phenomena such as simultaneous inventions (developed spontaneously and independently in different places at about the same time), re-inventions of lost techniques, 'alternative' inventions coming very close together in time for providing different ways of getting the same thing done.[3]

The 'profile' of technical change usually shows an evolutionary curve as well as revolutionary discontinuities. The interstices between the discrete advances made by identifiable individuals are filled by 'continuum' improvements made on the job, by countless improvements without known, or identifiable and published authorship. Collectively the latter may yield a cumulative advance in productivity greater than the identifiable discrete innovations. This has been likened to biological change, improvement and survival by the techniques most efficiently and economically adapted to their function – a kind of technological Darwinism.[4] The burden of all this is, of course, that invention waits upon economic opportunity before it can come to fruition in innovation and the diffusion of new techniques. The determinants of timing are usually set – in the long run – by non-technical criteria. These determinants may be economic criteria of different sorts – the widening of the market giving inducement for larger production

---

1 Surveying techniques were certainly advanced enough in the late sixteenth century to facilitate canal cutting. The New River project bringing water from Hertfordshire to North London involved very sophisticated routing and exactness in calculating levels.

2 A. R. Hall and T. S. Kuhn in M. Clagett, *Critical Problems in the History of Science* (Madison, Wisc., 1959), pp. 16–17.

3 R. K. Merton, 'Singletons and Multiples in Scientific Discovery', *Proceedings of the American Philosophical Society*, cv (1961); W. R. Maclaurin, 'The Sequence from Invention to Innovation ... ', *Quarterly Journal of Economics*, lxvii (1953).

4 S. C. Gilfillan, *The Sociology of Invention* (Chicago, 1935); 'Invention as a Factor in Economic History', *Journal of Economic History*, Supplement (1945).

and hence new methods, greater facility in the supply of capital, a change in factor prices[1] (for example, labour becoming relatively more expensive or intractable, raising the incentives to cut labour costs). Boom conditions, creating bottle necks in supply, higher profits, and greater incentives to expand may create the operational incentives. In a dynamic sequence, when an economy is on the move with innovations flowing, a depression may equally induce further innovation by creating pressures to cut costs. The process of innovation itself creates a dis-equilibrium in various ways – that dis-equilibrium, to be resolved, creating the need for further changes, which become self-reinforcing. These may indeed be technical in nature, but they are need-creating in the way they operate. The causal arrows flow from industrial demand towards the absorption of new knowledge. The timing is set from within the industrial rhythm and the economic context, rather than given to it exogenously by new acquisitions of knowledge.[2] There are other determinants – social, political and legal – affecting the condition of risk. 'Entrepreneurship' may also prove to be greater than the sum of these other criteria.

These sorts of motivations tend to be the operational criteria in this period, I believe, determining which bits of scientific knowledge were taken up, developed, applied, and which lay unused; which inventions remained known, but sterile, and which quickly became adopted, perhaps outside the country which gave them birth. Clearly, this is the style of explanation

---

[1] 'Every price change, by creating cost difficulties in certain fields and opportunities for profit making in others, provides a double stimulus to invention.' (A. Plant in *Economica* (1934), 38, quoted Clark, *Science and Social Welfare*.)

[2] J. Schmookler, *Invention and Economic Growth* (Cambridge, Mass. 1966); 'Economic Sources of Inventive Activity', *Journal of Economic History*, XXII (1962); W. F. Osburn and D. Thomas, 'Are Inventions Inevitable?', *Political Science Quarterly*, XXXVII (1922); R. C. Epstein, 'Industrial Inventions: Heroic or Systematic?' *Quarterly Journal of Economics*, XL (1926); R. K. Merton, 'Fluctuations in the Rate of Industrial Invention', *Quarterly Journal of Economics*, XLIX (1934–5).

The very large literature about technical change and innovation now developing is seeking to establish criteria for measuring and evaluating this phenomenon in economic theory. Almost all of it relates to twentieth-century examples and assumptions, particularly that concerned with research costs and applied science. Conclusions are therefore not *ipso facto* applicable to innovation as a phenomenon in the seventeenth and eighteenth centuries.

behind the very rapid adoption of 'chemical' bleaching in the cotton industry in Britain more than in France: the enormous expansion in the output of cloth made a more rapid means of bleaching imperative. Great stress has recently been placed by historians of science on the ways in which empirical processes and skilled artisan technology in the mechanical arts stimulated scientific advance in these centuries.[1]

This does not, however, necessarily subvert the core of the 'positive' equation. It can be argued that applied science needs to build up a capital 'stock' or a 'library' of knowledge, so to speak, which is thereupon available for industrialists to draw upon in innovation – across national frontiers, no doubt, for science now enjoyed, in printing, a very effective means of diffusing knowledge in the seventeenth century and after; and with a timing doubtless profoundly influenced by conditions and incentives within industry. But, without that capital stock produced by the advance of scientific knowledge, runs the argument, a limit would have been placed upon the range of advance.

This begs a question as to how far the impetus deriving from industry was able to produce the conditions – of innovation as well as other things – needed to sustain its own progress. To what extent was the flow of innovations produced from within the empirical world of industry and not given to it from an 'exogenous' world of science, advancing under its own complex of stimuli? That in turn begs the question as to how far industrial demand, with the needs of the 'empirical' world, was itself the stimulus for creating new scientific knowledge in this period, of what 'feeds-back' or 'feeds-forward' there were?

Judging the effectiveness of the contributions of science by results, *ex post facto*, rather than by endeavour, is to greatly reduce their importance. Little of the mass of experimentation

[1] E.g. P. Rossi, *Francis Bacon* (London, 1968), p. 9; E. J. Dijksterhuis, *The Mechanisation of the World Picture* (Oxford, 1961), pp. 243-4; T. S. Kuhn, 'Energy Conservation ... ' in Clagett, *Critical Problems in the History of Science;* A. R. Hall, *From Galileo to Newton, 1630-1720* (London, 1963), pp. 329-43; A. R. Hall, *The Scientific Revolution* (London, 2nd ed. 1962), pp. 221, 225, 236; J. D. Bernal, *Science in History* (London, 1954), pp. 345-6, 371. At its extreme, this case becomes the doctrinaire Marxist position that advances in scientific knowledge were determined purely by the bourgeoisie's commercial and industrial needs. See B. Hessen, *Science at the Cross-Roads* and the debate given in condensed form in G. Basalla (ed.), *The Rise of Modern Science* (Boston, 1968).

in agricultural projects of the Royal Society in its early years, for example, seems to have had much direct effect upon improving the efficiency of farming.[1] Most of the more direct links between advancing knowledge of chemistry and the expanding chemical industry came only at the end of the eighteenth century. This disconnects the timing of much of the new knowledge, particularly in chemistry, from the initial phases of industrial growth. The great advances in mechanics in the seventeenth century – then one of the most advanced of the sciences – had given birth to very sophisticated theoretical schema about ballistics, which do not appear to have significantly affected the processes of innovation in making metals or working metals, of gunfounding or of gunnery, again judging by results, until after the Crimean War. The 'science' remained almost purely abstract. Each cannon cast and bored remained slightly different from every other; each shot and each charge of powder were equally 'unique', which kept techniques of gunnery strictly empirical. A precision engineering industry to produce the guns, and a precision chemical industry to produce the propellants, were required before this theoretical knowledge could become operational.[2]

The empirical stimulus creating response within the immediate context of production accounts for a very high proportion of the advance in productivity, even in those industries most exposed to the impact of science, and a great determinant of timing and the rate of diffusion of new techniques. Great areas of advance were relatively untouched by scientific knowledge, judging by result rather than by intention or endeavour, until the nineteenth century: agriculture, canals, machine-making, the mechanisation of cloth-making (as distinct from bleaching and dyeing), iron- and steel-making. Taking the occupational census of 1851, a very small percentage indeed of the labour-force was engaged in trades where the linkages were – superficially at any rate – high, as in chemicals.

IV

Steam power is important enough to merit separate attention.

[1] See below, pp. 73–6.
[2] A. R. Hall, *Ballistics in the Seventeenth Century* (Cambridge, 1952).

Here was the greatest gift from science to industry, it has often been claimed, born exactly from the world of the Royal Society, of noblemen's laboratories, from an international competition amongst scientists and their leisured patrons in the seventeenth century. Watt, in his generation, carried on this precise linkage between scientific knowledge and commercial application in the series of formal experiments to analyse the properties of steam and the conductivity of metals which lay behind his own inventions of the separate condenser and steam power proper (as distinct from 'atmospheric' power). This can be called the classical example of science in alliance with practice. But other factors also conditioned the rates of advance of efficiency in steam power and the timing of stages of growth of this innovation. Thomas Newcomen and Savery were not so directly within this educated scientific tradition. And historians of science continue to push back the genealogy of the basic scientific awareness of steam power – knowledge as distinct from laboratory experiments that worked.[1] The jump to the world of Thomas Newcomen, who had no personal contacts with the leading scientists of the day,[2] fashioning an effective commercial device, meant problems of manufacture, of standards of accuracy in metalworking, that alone made effective use possible on a commercial basis. This, it can be argued, more than anything else set the limits of efficiency. And this, as a blacksmith, was Newcomen's world, not that of the Royal Society. Once again, the context within which Watt's inventions had to become operational meant that the accuracy of working metal, of fitting a piston to a cylinder throughout its length, of getting steam-proof valves and joints set the limits to the rise in the degree of efficiency which potentially resulted from the new inventions. These efficiencies came from the empirical world of John Wilkinson and Matthew Boulton, with rising standards of its own, a world increasingly working to rule, but still mainly innocent of formal scientific thought.

[1] A. R. Hall has gone so far as to state: 'No scientific revolution was needed to bring the steam engine into existence. What Newcomen did could have been done by Hero of Alexandria seventeen hundred years before, who understood all the essential principles' (*From Galileo to Newton, 1630–1720* (London, 1963), p. 333).

[2] D. S. L. Cardwell, *Steampower in the Eighteenth Century* (London, 1963), p. 18.

And, subsequent to Watt, most of the pioneering of 'high-pressure steam', the adaptation of steam to traction, to small-bench engines, to ships and the continuum of improvement to the Watt-style engine itself, belonged, for the most part, to the empirical world of the obscure colliery engineers, the captains of Cornish mines, the brilliant mechanics such as Murdock. Some of them were trained in the best precision workshops of the country, such as Maudslay's, but remained nevertheless innocent of scientific fundamentals and were not seeking to create their improvements in the light of awareness of such fundamentals. Yet the cumulative total effects of 'continuum' innovation, effected on the job, at the work bench, bit by bit, were profound. Taking steam-power efficiency again as one example, the first Newcomen engine had a duty[1] of *circa* 4.5 m., it has been calculated.[2] This had been raised to 12.5 m. by the time of Smeaton's improvements in 1770. The initial Watt separate condenser engine raised this duty to *c.* 22 m. By 1792 it had been raised by continuing improvement to over 30 m. The best recorded Watt-type engine in 1811, working in Cornwall, had a duty of 22.3 m. In 1842–3, under continuous gradual improvement, the best duty was recorded at 100 m. Average duty rates recorded on Cornish engines quadrupled between 1811 and 1850 as a result of this continuum-type improvement.

V

Although this essay is primarily concerned with sources of innovation in industrial techniques, improvements in agriculture are relevant to the issue, both because agriculture potentially stood to gain from the application of science, comparably to industry (and has gained as dramatically from its connection with science as has industry in the twentieth century), and because contemporaries certainly gave agricultural improvement at least as high a priority as industrial

---

[1] The number of pounds of water raised one foot by the consumption of 1 bushel of coal.

[2] D. B. Barton, *The Cornish Beam Engine* (Truro, 1966), pp. 28, 32, 58. These figures are suspect, but there is no reason to suppose that the degree of suspicion advanced with time – rather the reverse. Other factors went into these duty counts as well as the intrinsic technical potentiality of the engines.

advance. Agricultural improvement also had a more general appeal to the upper and middle-classes of English society than any other branch of production, if only because larger and more influential social groups were concerned with the land. Agricultural innovations and scientific experiments in agriculture featured in virtually all the scientific and philosophical societies mentioned above; while other societies were specifically agricultural in their terms of reference. The Georgical Committee of the Royal Society was established in 1665 (as one of eight sectoral groups). Many experiments in husbandry found a place in the *Philosophical Transactions* over the years; and eleven reports are known to have been made about agricultural practices, produced from national enquiries.[1] A 'Society of Improvers in the Knowledge of Agriculture in Scotland' was founded in 1723 (forty years before that in Brecknockshire) and many local agricultural societies followed, particularly in the 1790s.[2]

Scientists concerned themselves with agricultural experiments, advocating the experimental method and lauding the claims of science in farming no less than in industry. Francis Bacon's *Sylva Sylvarum* (1651) included a comparative study of different modes of fertilising. In 1671, Boyle urged farmers to experiment. 'Chymical experiments . . .' he wrote, 'may probably afford useful directions to the Husbandman towards the melioration of his land, both for Corn, Trees, Grass and consequently Cattell.'[3] John Evelyn's various works contained a curious – if typical – mixture of magic and shrewd commonsense, in circumstances where virtually anything organic, and much inorganic, could be thrown onto the land with advantage.[4] Hale's *Vegetable Statics* (1727) continued the line, for the first time challenging the view that plants were composed simply of water. Francis Home, both a doctor and subsequently a professor in Edinburgh, also deliberately set

[1] R. L. Lennard, 'Agriculture under Charles II', *Economic History Review* (1932).
[2] These include the Canterbury Agricultural Society, Odiham Society, London Veterinary College, Bath and West and Southern Counties, Norfolk Agricultural Society.
[3] R. Boyle, *Some Considerations Touching the Usefulness of . . . Natural Philosophy* (Oxford, 1671).
[4] J. Evelyn, *Sylva* (London, 1644); *Kalendarium Hortense* (London, 1664); *A Philosophical discourse of earth . . .* (London, 1676).

out to apply science to agriculture to see 'how far Chymistry could go in settling the Principles of Agriculture'.[1] Lavoisier set up agricultural experiments and ran a model farm.[2]

Thus, taking the evidence of intention and endeavour, agricultural innovation shares with industry a common link with science in the seventeenth and eighteenth centuries. The problems about concluding from these aspirations and associations that applied science was the prime source of such innovation in agriculture as actually occurred are even greater, if anything, than with industry. There, at least, in the specialised sector of the chemical industry and immediately related fields there is solid evidence for the connection in a direct way (though casual links could flow in both directions). Much theorising was plainly mistaken, based on quite irrational premises. The innovations which characterised progressive farming did not owe much, if anything, to such science; while only the very exceptional farmer or landowner was directly influenced by the scientists. Russell, as a leading present-day agricultural scientist is profoundly sceptical of the relevance of chemistry to agricultural advance before the generation of Leibig, Davy's *Elements of Agricultural Chemistry* (1813) and the Rothamsted experiments of Lawes and Gilbert in the 1840s.[3]

But scepticism about the significance of the direct application of formal scientific knowledge to agrarian improvement in these two centuries does not end the story of the relevance of this evidence. To anticipate a tentative conclusion drawn below, one can certainly take this large body of data as strong evidence of *motivation* for agrarian advance. Coupled with false premises about chemical reactions were urgent pleas for experimentation, shrewd observation and recording, the comparative method, seeking alternative ways of doing things which could be measured and tested to see if they were superior to the old. This was a programme for rejecting traditional methods justifiable only because things had always

[1] F. Home, *Principles of Agriculture and Vegetation* (Edinburgh, 1757).
[2] E. J. Russell, *A History of Agricultural Science in Great Britain, 1620–1954* (London, 1966), p. 53.
[3] E. J. Russell, *A History of Agricultural Science*, pp. 25, 37, 46. See also G. E. Fussell, 'Science and Practice in Eighteenth Century British Agriculture', *Agricultural History*, XLIII (1969). But see the comments of D. J. Brandenburg.

been done in that way (even though such customs, hallowed by the passing of time, often did embody strict rationality, even if unselfconscious and inarticulate on the lips of their practitioners). Scientific procedures and attitudes encouraged by the scientists may have been more influential than the scientific knowledge they dispensed. 'I should not, therefore, proceed a single step', wrote Francis Home, 'without facts and experiments.'[1]

The publicity given to new methods, new crops, rotations and implements by these same groups may also have increased the pace of diffusion of innovations in agriculture. Certainly the flood of writings, at all different levels, is evidence of an intellectual world where progress was written into the assumptions of the age.

VI

The institutional development of science creates certain problems, because the patterns of development in science do not always fit sequences of innovation and development in industry. The foundation of the Royal Society and the Lunar Society are always quoted as evidence of the developing nexus between science and industry. But one must then face the issue of the decline in the utilitarian orientation towards applied science of the Royal Society after 1670, its decline during the first half of the eighteenth century and in parts of the nineteenth century, and its great weaknesses compared with the equivalent academy in France. The Lunar Society also withered into a state of collapse after the seventeen-nineties. In some fields also it seems perfectly possible – even in that most applied of sciences, medicine – for the accumulated advances of several generations, well institutionalised, not to result in any major impact upon national demographic trends in death-rates or disease-rates. Medicine, we are told, did not begin to have such a major impact – that is, upon a statistically significant proportion of the population – until the second half of the nineteenth century, apart, perhaps, from the effects of inoculation and vaccination on smallpox. And this was in a

[1] F. Home, *Principles of Agriculture and Vegetation* (Edinburgh, 1757). He urged the Edinburgh Society to raise 'a spirit of experimental farming over the country'.

field where there was very great interest, considerable advances in scientific knowledge, a greater flow of money, and probably more scientifically trained persons than in all other branches of science put together.[1]

The problem of numbers is also relevant. Persons professionally trained in medicine, in chemistry, the 'scientific' members of the Royal Society (as distinct from the much larger number of 'gentlemen' innocent of professional commitment) remained the merest handful. The average number of elections to the Royal Society in the early eighteenth century was about ten. The average number elected in each year to the College of Physicians was five or six before 1700, supplemented only marginally with those with degrees from foreign universities. These numbers did rise after 1700 but remained very tiny. This may be taken as an index of the professionalisation of science to the extent that this term possessed its modern connotation in the eighteenth century. Beyond this there were, of course, much larger numbers of amateurs and people in business, such as opticians and distillers, who practised empirical science in a commercial way. As Professor Hall has said:

the impact of any question of abstract science upon a human brain was exceptionally infrequent – it could only happen to, say, one individual in a hundred thousand. But, in the history of technology the situation is very different; the proportion of human beings who could have been very well acquainted with handmills and ploughs and textile- and horsegear has always been very large indeed, until the last century or so in the West. Very few of these ever effected the slightest variation in any technique; but the potentiality for effecting a variation was virtually universal. It is only when the use of relatively uncommon machines or techniques is introduced that the potentiality for innovation becomes restricted.[2]

In England no great expansion of institutions in 'professional' science developed in this period outside the Royal Society, either within the universities or outside them, apart from the amateur groups and the popularisers. Science did not become an established part of the educational system, either within the traditional institutional hierarchy or beyond it in special organisations of its own. The Mechanics' Institutes subsequently

---

[1] This conclusion may need to be modified in the light of research being currently undertaken by Dr E. Sigsworth of York. See below, pp. 97–110.
[2] A. R. Hall, *The Historical Relations of Science and Technology* (London, 1963).

became the only widespread national movement to get institutionalised in this way in the first half of the nineteenth century, and they trained the aspiring literate artisan, not the research chemist. The greatest contrast existed between the English experience and French and German developments in the *École Polytechnique* and the *Technische Hochschule*. The School of Mines and the Royal College of Chemistry in London were the two institutions that challenged this generalisation. They remained very small, isolated geographically, socially and technically from having any significant impact upon mining or industry in Britain as a whole during the first half of the nineteenth century.

VII

In conclusion: it was the same Western European society which saw both great advances in science and in technological change in the great sweep of time and region across the fifteenth to the nineteenth centuries. It would be carrying nihilism to the point of dogma to write this off as a mere accident, even though the case of China suggests that it is perfectly possible for sophisticated scientific and technological knowledge in some fields to produce a very small impetus towards lifting general levels of industrial technique. The simplest assumptions of causation flowing directly and in one direction need to be questioned; the presumption that connections between science and industry were direct, unitary, simple. Negatively it can be argued that the many other conditioning factors in technical change were collectively of much greater importance during the first century of industrialisation and that, in the immediate context of manufacture, formal scientific knowledge was much less strategic in determining commercial success than some modern studies have suggested. In longer perspective we may see that the main impetus from formal applied science to innovation came after 1850 on an ever widening front, but in a context which was highly favourable for many other reasons. That this was the real pivot in the connections between science and industry was shown by default, to a large extent, in the case of Britain lagging most in exactly those fields of innovation where the connection was becoming most intimate.

But much depends upon whether we are looking at the immediate context of innovation or at the general nature of the society, and its intellectual parameters, within which industrial advances were burgeoning. 'We have to see', as Sir George Clark concluded, 'not a gradual and general mutual approach of these elements in society, but the joining of contact, first at isolated points, then at more points; finally almost everywhere.'[1] Until the end of the eighteenth century – that is, until long after systematic, cumulative change on a scale quite uncharacteristic of medieval technical change was under way – that inter-penetration was confined to fairly small areas, even if some of them were strategic.

It should also be acknowledged that scientific attitudes were much more widespread and diffused than scientific knowledge. Attitudes of challenging traditional intellectual authority, deciding lines of development by observation, testing, experimentation and adopting – indeed, actively stimulating the development of – scientific devices such as the thermometer and hydrometer, which enabled industrialists to reduce their empirical practices to rule wherever possible, were certainly being strengthened.[2] The quest for more exact measurement and research for the means to fulfil it was certainly characteristic of these linkages, even where the object was not to subvert empirical techniques, of which the chemistry remained unknown, but to standardise best practice within them. Scientific devices and techniques were thus often used to buttress empirical techniques rather than to challenge them. In this sense, the developing Baconian tradition of the experimental sciences, the tradition of research based upon systematic experimentation (as in late-eighteenth-century chemistry) had closer links with the process of innovation than did advances in cosmology, mechanics or physics in the seventeenth century. And in such linkages science probably learned as much from technology as technology from science until the nineteenth century: scientists were much concerned with trying to answer questions suggested from industrial

[1] Clark, *Science and Social Welfare*, p. 22.
[2] The brewing and distilling industries, with the excise authorities anxious to have more precise calculations in gauging for taxation, offer a good example of such a sequence. See P. Mathias, *The Brewing Industry in England, 1700–1830* (Cambridge, 1959), pp. 63–78.

techniques. 'Technological progress implied the idea of intellectual progress, just as chance discoveries implied the possibility of systematic ones.'[1]

We may conclude that together both science and technology give evidence of a society increasingly curious, increasingly questing, increasingly on the move, on the make, having a go, increasingly seeking to experiment, wanting to improve. This may be the prime significance of the new popularisers of science and technology, the encyclopaedias, the institutions like the Society of Arts, the Royal Institution, the Lunar Society and the various local philosophical and scientific societies, the new educational movements, the intriguing links between radical non-conformist scientific and business groups in the eighteenth century or between Puritans and the founders of the Royal Society in the seventeenth century. So much of the significance, that is to say, impinges at a more diffused level, affecting motivations, values, assumptions, the mode of approach to problem-solving, the intellectual milieu, rather than a direct transference of knowledge. In this sense, of course, the conclusion is banal, that the advances in science and in technical change should both be seen as characteristics of that society, not one being simply consequential upon the other.

[1] A. R. Hall, *The Scientific Revolution* (London, 1962), p. 369.

4

SCIENCE AND THE STEAM ENGINE,
1790–1825[1]

by D. S. L. Cardwell

The year 1969 marked the bicentenary of two most important events in world history: the granting of a patent to Richard Arkwright for his water-frame, by means of which the skilled craft of spinning was at last mechanised, and of a patent to James Watt for his condensing steam engine. The connection between these two events and the progress of physical science is not at all obvious. Indeed, the suggestion that any advance in technology can determine the progress of science has been explicitly denied by a number of recent writers. It is the purpose of this essay to try to refute this view, at least as regards one very important and satisfyingly fundamental branch of science on the one hand and the power technologies on the other.

Although we are concerned with the steam engine and its consequences for science it is not possible to avoid some discussion of the other power technologies and in particular that of water. The reason is very simple: there was strong cross-fertilisation between the various power technologies; the men who designed and built steam engines usually concerned themselves with water-power also and the devices and techniques of the one art were often borrowed by the other. In the end, as we shall show, a successful attempt was made to apply the basic principles of the older technology to the newer.

The eighteenth century was the heyday of water-power technology; the time when it achieved not only a degree of mechanical sophistication but a sound theoretical basis as well. For it was during the eighteenth century that the ideas worked out by the mechanical philosophers of the 'scientific revolution' were first applied in the field of power technology. Galileo

---

[1] Certain of the ideas discussed in this paper are dealt with at greater length in the author's *Watt to Clausius* (London, 1971).

had realised that in a perfect, friction-free machine there is no loss of 'force', so that the effort put in must equal the useful effect obtained. This advance made possible such eighteenth and early nineteenth-century measures as 'duty', horse-power and work and it contributed to the development of the idea of energy.

The quantification of power and the correlative idea that the efficiency of a machine – or a process – can be expressed as a simple numerical fraction was a fundamental advance. A given amount of water flowing in a stream, if diverted smoothly upwards to make a fountain, or *jet d'eau*, reaches the height from which it falls; or rather it should do so, according to Galileo, if there is no friction and no air resistance. The efficiency of a water engine applied to this stream is, expressed numerically, the ratio of the weight it can lift to the height from which the water falls to the total weight of water falling. This fraction must always be less than 1; for a perfect engine it would be exactly 1: such a machine could deliver just enough power to enable a (perfect) pump to restore all the water to the source. An efficiency greater than 1 would, of course, imply 'perpetual motion'; that is, a continuous useful effect without any expenditure of effort.

It was in 1704 that the first calculation of the efficiency of a machine – an 'undershot' waterwheel – was published.[1] The fraction, $\frac{4}{27}$, was surprisingly low, for the machine was supposed to be free of all losses; but the author, Antoine Parent, had unwittingly made certain assumptions which seriously limited its generality. These limitations were, in effect, eliminated by the Chevalier Déparcieux (1752) and John Smeaton (1759).

It is a very natural assumption, based on common experience, that the performance of a great deal of work must be accompanied by outwards and manifest evidence: groans and sweat in the case of humans and animals; creaks, vibrations and noise in the case of all mechanical agents. Thus, to a child a paddle steamer which churns up a great deal of froth and turbulence would seem to be exerting a great deal more power than a screw steamer which hardly disturbs the water at all.

Smeaton, an engineer who had had a great deal of practical

---

[1] Antoine Parent, 'Sur la Plus Grande Perfection des Machines', *Histoire et Mémoires de l'Académie Royale des Sciences* (1704), pp. 144, 432.

experience, saw the fallacy in this plausible, 'commonsense', view.[1] The turbulence and spray produced when a stream of water strikes against the blades of an undershot waterwheel indicates power being *wasted*; power which applied more efficiently could lift an additional weight and not, as he put it, 'distort the figure of the stream'. He therefore recommended that waterwheels be either 'overshot', with buckets round the rim so that water passing over the top filled the buckets and acted by weight rather than impact, or that they be at any rate 'breast wheels'. The latter represented a compromise between the undershot and overshot modes and was particularly suitable for large streams or rivers with relatively gentle gradients: instead of striking the blades underneath the wheel the water was raised by a weir so that it entered the machine at axle height and so acted by weight rather than by impact. Breast wheels became very common after Smeaton's time; and it was men brought up in the principles he had established, engineers like Ewart, Hewes and Fairbairn, who designed the great waterwheels that drove the mills and factories of early industrial England.[2]

As one might have expected the formal, or mathematical, statement of the conditions under which water power is best transformed into useful mechanical power was first made by two Frenchmen: the Chevalier de Borda and Lazare Carnot.[3] In 1767 Borda pointed out that for the maximum useful power the water must enter the machine without shock or impact so that no energy (*vis-viva* in the thought and language of those times) is lost in causing turbulence and spray and that it must leave without appreciable velocity; for evidently if water comes jetting out of a machine it must be carrying so much energy with it. Borda went on to suggest that, in the case of undershot waterwheels the blades should be curved, pointing upstream to minimise the shock of impact and to reverse the flow of water

---

[1] John Smeaton, 'An Experimental Enquiry concerning the Natural Powers of Wind and Water ... ', *Phil. Trans. Roy. Soc.* LI (1759), 100.

[2] Dr A. J. Pacey and Mr S. B. Smith have carried out detailed studies of these large waterwheels and of the engineers who designed them. See S. B. Smith, *Thomas Cheek Hewes, an ingenious engineer and mechanic of Manchester*, M.Sc. Thesis, University of Manchester (1969).

[3] Chevalier de Borda, 'Sur les Roues Hydrauliques', *A.R. de S.* (1767), 149, 270; Lazare Carnot, *Essai sur les machines en général* (Paris, 1783).

when it leaves the wheels. Borda was therefore the inventor of the principle of the turbine, but he is not usually given any credit for this.

Lazare Carnot established and confirmed Borda's dictum that the water must enter without shock and leave without appreciable velocity if the maximum amount of mechanical effort is to be transformed into useful effect and he did this in the context of a general theory of *vis-viva*. The conclusion in which all these writers concurred was that the theoretical maximum of efficiency for an overshot wheel would be 1, while for an undershot wheel it would be $\frac{1}{2}$, the difference being due to the fact that the former type could be made to satisfy the two basic conditions while the latter type could not (at least, unless curved blades were used).

According to these principles, arrived at experimentally and empirically in England and theoretically in France, every drop of water falling every inch could, ideally at any rate, be made to yield all its energy to a machine. This was singularly opportune for the industrial revolution which was then getting under way in England.

There is some evidence to suggest that there was at this time a growing power shortage in England. There was not, of course, a general power shortage, for the generation of power was an entirely local matter, but it was one which affected certain sectors of what were, by then, growth industries. In cotton textiles, for example, the biggest and best mills would inevitably be on the best sites of the best streams. As the industry developed, as markets expanded, capital was ploughed back and new high production machines were installed so more power was required. Before very long economic growth was putting a strain on the power resources of important and progressive sectors of the textile industry. Sir Richard Arkwright's inventions had put a premium on the more efficient generation (and use) of power.

Accordingly great – and at times almost desperate – ingenuity was shown in efforts to supplement, and even dispense with, the power of local streams. Dr Richard Hills has pointed out[1] that in 1788 there were about twenty-five cotton mills in Oldham parish, eleven of them being in the town of Oldham

[1] R. L. Hills, *Power in the Industrial Revolution* (Manchester, 1969).

itself; three years later, in 1791, the number in Oldham town had risen to eighteen. But because the best water sites had already been taken most of these mills were worked by horses.

Typical of many early cotton mills was that put up by Samuel Greg at Styal, in Cheshire, in 1784. A small waterwheel took power from the river Bollin but as the business expanded it was found to be inadequate. In 1796 Peter Ewart, a distinguished engineer and a close friend of the scientist John Dalton, was taken into partnership by Greg and the improvement of the mill initiated. A dam was built and a large and efficient breast wheel with cast iron axle and frame was designed and installed. In 1800 a Boulton and Watt steam engine was installed to supplement the waterwheel as required.[1]

The continued improvement of the industrial waterwheel had the effect of deferring the ultimate triumph of the steam engine by many years.[2] In some cases, in fact, the waterwheel retired undefeated. At Styal, for example, the waterwheel continued in use until the end of the nineteenth century; thereafter it was replaced by a water turbine which powered the mill until it closed down in 1939.

The steam engine had nevertheless been improved enormously since the original invention by Thomas Newcomen in 1712. In Newcomen's atmospheric engine a large metal cylinder fitted with a piston was filled with steam which was then condensed by a spray of cold water; a vacuum was thereby created in the cylinder and the pressure of the atmosphere outside drove the piston to the bottom of the cylinder. The steam supply was then turned on again, the piston was lifted by a counterweight and the procedure repeated. The engine was a heavy consumer of coal for every time the cylinder was filled with steam it had also to be heated up since steam in contact with cold metal condenses. This diseconomy meant that the engine could only be used where coal was plentiful or where there was an overriding necessity for power at all costs, as in the non-ferrous metal mining area of Cornwall.

It was James Watt who initiated the process of quantification by diagnosing that far more heat was being consumed in

---

[1] Frances Collier, *The family economy of the working classes in the cotton industry, 1784–1833* (Manchester, 1964), p. 38.

[2] The useful expression 'industrial waterwheel' has been coined by Dr A. J. Pacey.

warming up the cylinder than in filling it with steam, so that if this could be avoided or minimised a substantial economy would result. Watt's analysis, incidentally, presupposed two important advances which had just been made by his friend and mentor, Joseph Black: the invention of the concept of *quantity* of heat and the correlative measure of the specific heat capacity. Watt solved the problem of heat economy by inventing an engine with two cylinders; one, in which the piston moved, was kept hot all the time, while the other, in which the condensing spray operated, was kept cold all the time. The two cylinders were connected by a pipe with a stopcock so that when it was time to condense the steam the stopcock had only to be opened and all the steam would rush from the working cylinder into the cold one and there be condensed.

The invention of the true steam engine followed logically from Watt's desire to prevent cold air cooling the inside walls of the working cylinder and so wasting heat. Hot steam, at atmospheric pressure, would be just as effective mechanically as cold air and would obviate such heat losses.

In this way the true steam engine was developed from the Newcomen engine. The full range of Watt's genius, however, only became apparent when he followed up his initial invention with such innovations as the parallel motion, the sun-and-planet gear and the double-acting principle which enabled the steam engine to drive rotative machinery as well as the reciprocating pumps to which it had previously been restricted. Hardly less important – or revealing – was his invention of the principle of expansive operation.

In principle expansive operation was analogous to the second of the two Borda–Carnot conditions for water engines: the water must not leave the machine with appreciable velocity.[1] If we imagine steam at boiler pressure leaving the cylinder and flowing into the condenser we realise at once that it must do so with gale force, rushing madly down the pipe into the void of the condenser. This gale of steam represented, to a systematic technologist like Watt, a very serious loss of 'duty'.

---

[1] Watt's discovery of the expansive principle was announced in a letter to his friend Dr Small written on 28 May 1769. (Copy in Boulton and Watt Collection, Central Reference Library, Birmingham.) Regrettably, it is improbable that Watt had read, or even knew of Borda's paper at this time.

To avoid it he proposed to use the steam *expansively*: that is, he turned off the steam before the piston had gone far down the cylinder. The trapped steam continued to drive the piston down, for its pressure, although falling steadily as the volume increased, would be greater than that of the void. Ideally, to squeeze the last drop of duty out of a given quantity of steam it should be allowed to expand until its pressure is no greater than that of the vacuum: but this would require an impracticably long cylinder. Nevertheless, the principle of expansive operation indicated how ultimate economy of working could be obtained: a squirt of steam allowed to expand as much as possible until its pressure had fallen almost to zero.

Thus Watt who started out as an instrument maker and scientist and ended as an engineer and business man had made his immense and perceptive contributions to the development of steam power. On one point he had been adamantly conservative; he refused all his life to countenance the use of high pressure steam, believing – probably correctly for most of the time – that contemporary metallurgy could not guarantee boilers that would stand up to high pressures and high temperatures. Such was Watt's technological supremacy and his command of the steam engine business that during the period when his patents ran, from 1770 to 1800, the development of the high-pressure steam engine was virtually impossible. But as soon as his dominance ended the exploitation of high pressure steam became possible.

Broadly speaking the development of the steam engine after 1800 was along two different paths. On the one hand the small, compact and powerful high-pressure steam engines invented by Trevithick and Oliver Evans offered far greater flexibility. For if the pressure was sufficiently great the condensing cylinder, or condenser, could be dispensed with, the loss of efficiency being compensated by diminished heat losses from a smaller bulk, reduced friction losses and lower prime cost. Such simple and efficient engines could be put on four wheels to make a road or rail locomotive. The other main path of development was more in accord with the established tradition: moderately high-pressure beam engines working expansively and with a condenser. These big stationary engines, used

D. S. L. Cardwell

mainly in the mining and textile industries, became progressively more efficient throughout the nineteenth century.

The reciprocating beam engine was, however, not the only form of heat engine tried out over this period. On the contrary records show that a wide variety of different engines was tested with varying degrees of success. Some, like Kempelen's steam reaction engine, gave Watt cause for alarm. But Watt was able to 'prove' by egregiously mis-applying Parent's waterwheel theory, that Kempelen's engine could not be more efficient than his reciprocating engine with condenser.[1]

If a variety of engines was tried out so were several different 'working substances': solids, liquids and gases. Alcohol vapour and turpentine, however, offered no significant advantage over steam, and air proved too intractable: it was difficult to heat up and expanded only by one third over the same temperature rise that caused water to expand some 1,700 fold – that is, from cold water into steam.

In short the reciprocating steam engine won and it dominated nineteenth-century power technology until the advent of the steam turbine and gas and oil engines towards the end of the century. It enjoyed its long reign because it repeatedly proved its superiority over all other forms and all other working substances.

In the parallel technology, the waterwheel was almost equally supreme. The qualification is necessary because it did have a rival: an interesting hybrid, a product of cross-

---

[1] The application of Parent's theory to Kempelen's steam engines is described in a letter of 11 May, 1784 from Watt to Boulton (B. & W. Coll.). The late H. W. Dickinson thought, erroneously, that this indicated that Watt had conceived of the steam turbine. In fact, the theory of the turbine is built on the ruins of Parent's theory.

Watt justified the application of Parent's theory to Kempelen's engine on the grounds that the latter was, in effect, a steam-driven Barker's Mill. His source for this was almost certainly the account given in J. T. Desagulier's *A course of experimental philosophy*, vol. II (3rd ed. London, 1763), pp. 459ff. This describes tests with a model Barker's Mill which indicated that it did most work when moving at one-third of the speed of the water, in accordance with Parent's theory.

Ironically enough Barker's Mill does not work on the same principles as an undershot waterwheel and so Parent's theory – uncorrected or corrected (when the speed of the mill becomes one-half that of the water) – cannot be applied.

Watt refers, in this letter, to another theory which he can only partly understand but which gives him equal reassurance about the inadequacy of Kemplen's engine. It is quite possible that this was Borda's theory.

fertilisation between steam and water power. This was the column-of-water engine which, in effect, was a 'steam' engine driven by the pressure of water rather than that of steam.[1]

The development of the column-of-water engine followed closely on that of the steam engine. Double acting engines were developed, Watt's parallel motion was incorporated and ultimately even an analogue for expansive operation was devised. A large vessel connected to the high-pressure water pipe stored energy in the form of compressed air so that if the water was turned off early in the stroke the expanding air provided a steadily reducing pressure to complete the stroke. In this way much less energy was lost when the piston struck the bottom of the cylinder than would have been the case if the full pressure of the column of water had been behind it.

Parasitic on the superior geniuses of the steam engine designers the column-of-water engine designers achieved a creditable degree of efficiency and versatility. The engine could be used to provide power for pumping or for driving rotative machinery; some could even be reversed and used as pumps themselves. Moreover the engine could easily be operated within the Borda–Carnot conditions for optimum efficiency and it had one enormous advantage over the waterwheel. It was entirely flexible with respect to the head, or fall of water. A waterwheel can only use a fall equal to its own diameter, which in effect amounts to about forty feet. But a high pressure column-of-water engine could harness very much greater falls, the limit being set only by the pressure that the machine could stand. Indeed, by means of these engines the total fall of a stream from its source in the hills to the bottom of the valley could be efficiently exploited. Accordingly French engineers used to recommend that for falls up to forty feet waterwheels were best, but for falls greater than this column-of-water engines were to be preferred. Such machines had recorded efficiencies of something like 0.7.

One outstanding difference between this water engine and its parent the steam engine was that the water engine had behind it the systematic and exhaustive theory worked out by French mathematicians of the eighteenth century, while for the steam

---

[1] D. S. L. Cardwell, 'Power Technologies and the Advance of Science, 1700–1825', *Technology and Culture*, VI (1965), 188–207.

engine there was no comprehensive theory at all: no *general* theory, that is, of the principles and conditions under which heat produces mechanical effect.

In 1804 the Cornish engineer Arthur Woolf invented a form of expansive compound engine in which steam was allowed to expand in a small, high-pressure cylinder and was then released into another, bigger cylinder in which it expanded still further. The idea was not original but Woolf's engine proved very successful when it was introduced at the Wheal Abraham mine in 1816. It achieved a duty of something like 56 million ft/lbs per bushel; roughly twice that of the best Watt engines.

Now the accumulation of evidence after 1800 began to indicate that the high pressure engine might be more economical than the low pressure variety; but of course as it was almost impossible to compare one engine exactly with another this generalisation was hardly more than the opinion of experienced engineers. There were in fact, others who denied that the high pressure engine was superior in any other way than flexibility.[1]

In 1811 a very interesting project began. Every month the duty achieved by practically every engine in Cornwall was published in an impartial report.[2] This communal endeavour, which it was hoped would increase the efficiency of Cornish engines, went on year after year. Gradually a pattern was established which was independent of the qualities of any particular engine and of the claims of individual engineers. There seemed to be no doubt that, as a general rule, high pressure, expansively operated condensing engines were the most efficient and there seemed to be no evident limit to the duties that they might ultimately achieve. This pattern was duly noted by engineers and scientists in England and in France. Cornwall had, by now, the best steam power engineers in the world; this was confirmed when, under test conditions,

---

[1] The names of some of the engineers who were doubtful about the superiority of high-pressure steam engines may be found in the *Report from the select committee on steam boats ... with minutes of evidence*, House of Commons Papers (1813–17), 24 June, 1817.

[2] Summaries of the Monthly Reports were published in Tilloch's *Philosophical Magazine* and in *Annales de Chimie et de Physique*. There is a very useful account of the whole project in the *Historical statement of the steam engines in Cornwall* (London, 1839), written by the Lean brothers, the sons of the first 'reporter'.

the Fowey Consols engine achieved in 1834, a duty of 127 million ft/lbs per bushel of coal.

Contemporary physics could throw little light on this. Water, converted into steam increases its volume 1,700 times; in expanding the steam must do work against the atmospheric pressure of 15 lbs per square inch. Taking Davies Gilbert's figure for the amount of water that a bushel of good coal can evaporate this corresponds to a duty of about 50 million ft/lbs per bushel. Such an 'engine' is ideal in that it suffers no frictional losses and no allowance need be made for heat losses.[1] The trouble was that as early as 1816 Woolf's real and imperfect engine had exceeded this figure.

The Woolf engine had been taken to France by Humphrey Edwards and in that country it proved a great success; as Professor Landes has pointed out, its fuel economy was much appreciated in a country with little good coal.[2] French experience of high pressure, expansive engines was much the same as British although attempts to account for their superior duties were more sophisticated, reflecting the more advanced state of French mathematics. The consensus of opinion in France, as in England, was that superior efficiency resulted from expansive operation together with detailed improvement in engine design, boiler and furnace construction, careful attention to thermal lagging and improved valve mechanisms. Such was the opinion of, for example, S. D. Poisson, expressed in a paper of 1823 in which he also announced the familiar formula, $p.v^{\gamma} = \text{constant}$. However, some people thought there might still be a hidden factor in some way related to temperature, so that high pressure steam engines were basically more efficient.[3]

---

[1] If the steam is allowed to condense to form a void into which water can rise through a pipe from a well 32 feet below, then the duty performed will be equal to the quantity of water lifted multiplied by 32 for the amount of coal burned. This amounts, in effect, to an idealised Savery engine (1699); and 50 million ft/lbs per bushel represents the ultimate limit of efficiency of such machines which at best achieved a duty of about 5 million ft/lbs per bushel (John Farey, *A treatise on the steam engine* (London, 1827), gives details of the 'improved' Savery engine; see also Davies Gilbert, 'On the Expediency of ... a new Term in Mechanics', *Phil. Trans. Roy. Soc.* (1827), 25).

[2] David Landes, *Cambridge Economic History of Europe*, edited by M. M. Postan and H. J. Habbakuk, vol. VI, pt. I (1965), p. 410.

[3] Among those who thought that there might be an intrinsic connection between the temperature of steam and the work which an engine could perform were

An important axiom had been propounded by Peter Ewart in a long paper that he published in 1813.[1] A given amount of fuel produces a given amount of heat no matter how slowly or quickly it is burned; and to this amount of heat there must correspond a fixed amount of work. Although in actual practice we can never realise the full quantity of work from a given amount of heat there can be no doubt of the correspondence between the two. This axiom was an essential step towards Joule's doctrine of the mechanical equivalence of heat; but Ewart stated it in the context of the material, or 'caloric', theory of heat: equivalence does not necessarily mean conversion or transformation.

One man who accepted the material theory of heat and who thought that the analogies between water engines and steam engines could, and should, be used to establish a general theory of the heat engine in accordance with the experience gained by (mainly English) engineers was Sadi Carnot, the son of Lazare Carnot. He set out his preliminary ideas in a short book, which was to be his only published work, entitled *Réflexions sur la puissance motrice du feu* (1824).[2] Explicitly the young Carnot sought to do for heat engines what theorists like his father, had done for water engines; the result was a work which Sir Joseph Larmor described as one of the most original arguments in physical science.

Réflexions is, in fact, neither a text-book on heat nor a popular account of heat engines. It is, quite simply, a book which sets out a new cosmology: a cosmology of heat-mechanics, or, as that ardent disciple of Carnot, William Thomson (Lord Kelvin) later called it, 'thermodynamics'.

Heat, Carnot remarks, is the grand moving agent of the universe. It accounts for a vast range of natural phenomena: rainfall, ocean currents, even volcanoes and earthquakes. Man has learned to harness this agent and to use it to execute specific tasks measured in the commonly accepted units of work or

John Prideaux (*Annals of Philosophy*, x (1825), 432) and John Dalton (*Memoirs of the Manchester Literary and Philosophical Society*, 11 (1813), 1, note to article by John Sharpe).

[1] Peter Ewart, 'On the Measure of Moving Force', *Manchester Memoirs*, 11 (1813), 105.

[2] S. Carnot, *Réflexions sur la puissance motrice du feu* (Paris, 1824). See also *Reflections on the motive power of fire* (Dover Books, 1961), the translation by R. H. Thurston to which Professor Mendoza has added a useful introduction.

duty. Steam engines can pump thousands of tons of water from mines, they can saw wood, forge iron, drive cotton mills and even haul heavy trucks along prepared tracks.

The steam engine had thus led to a considerable extension of human experience of nature; the sort of experience on which science can be built. Through the steam engine we gain an insight into the mechanical effects of heat that we could not get from any other source, for nowhere else are they so manifest and dramatically obvious to the understanding.

Wherever, observes Carnot, there are two bodies at different temperatures, wherever there is a 'fall' of caloric, there is the possibility of producing motion, or doing work. A cold body, or condenser is as necessary as the hot body, or furnace, for without it there could be no work-producing flow of heat, or caloric. With the hydraulic analogy in mind Carnot then goes on to describe how a perfect engine, operating between two particular hot and cold bodies, could perform the maximum possible amount of useful work.[1] The first condition, exactly analogous to the Borda–Carnot conditions for water engines, is that when the working substance (the steam) absorbs heat it must do so at the same temperature as the hot body; when it gives up heat it must do so at the same temperature as the cold body. Watt's principle of expansive operation makes this possible; at least in theory. As the steam (or air or gas) in the cylinder expands so its temperature falls. This phenomenon, the 'adiabatic' cooling of an expanding gas had been discussed by Erasmus Darwin some forty years earlier and he had applied it to the explanation of certain climatological problems and even to the operation of his friend's, Mr Watt's, steam engine.[2]

Once the steam has expanded so much that its temperature is that of the cold body, or condenser, we must somehow restore the initial conditions so that the next cycle can begin. The obvious way of doing this would be to evaporate a little more water to provide the necessary steam, but this would violate the Carnot (junior) condition that there is no non-productive

[1] Dr A. J. Pacey points out that Watt's invention of the separate condenser, or cold body, made it much easier for Carnot to visualise the operation of an ideal engine. The necessity of the cold body is not nearly so obvious in the operation of a Trevithick-type high pressure steam engine without condenser.

[2] Erasmus Darwin, 'Frigorific Experiments on the Mechanical Expansion of Air', *Phil. Trans. Roy. Soc.* (1788), 43.

flow of heat. Practical engineers like Trevithick had already seen this point for they had made provision for the waste heat of exhaust steam to pre-heat the boiler feed-water.

Carnot's solution, although applicable to all types of engine, is more readily described if we restrict ourselves to air engines. The cold, expanded air at the temperature of the cold body is compressed while the cylinder is kept in contact with the cold body; it therefore gives up heat – caloric is squeezed out of it – to the latter and the temperature cannot rise. At a certain point the cold body is removed and the compression continues, the temperature now rising until it reaches that of the hot body. If we have chosen our compressions correctly the air will now be in exactly the same state as at the start – and the only net effect will have been the performance of work and the flow of a certain amount of heat through the engine from the hot to the cold body.

At every point in this cycle of operations the engine can be reversed so that it could act in effect like a pump – just as a mechanically perfect water engine can – and by being driven in this way it could restore heat to the hot body, or source. If it *were* possible to devise an even more efficient engine then it would only be necessary to use it to drive a Carnot engine in reverse to achieve perpetual motion.

Having carefully defined his perfect engine, Carnot next shows that no one working substance – air, steam, alcohol vapour, etc. – can be superior to any other; it is simply and solely the temperature difference which determines the amount of work which a unit of heat can perform. From the fact that all substances yield the same mechanical effect for the same fall of temperature Carnot draws a number of important conclusions about the physics of gases and vapours. He even saw that it might be possible to derive a temperature scale based not on the properties of particular substances but on the work done by a perfect heat engine.

The importance of all this for the future of physics (and chemistry) hardly needs to be underlined. But Carnot was concerned with technology as well as science. Why, he asked, were high-pressure steam engines more efficient than low-pressure ones? Ignoring suggestions that it was due to detailed improvement he seems to have relied on the hydraulic analogy and argued that just as the best water engine is one which harnesses the biggest fall, so the best heat engine will be one that can work over the biggest temperature difference. Now the temperature difference between burning coal and cold water is about 1,000 °C; of this difference the low-pressure steam engine can utilise less than 100°, but the high-pressure steam engine, whose steam temperature is considerably above 100° therefore makes proportionately greater use of the total 'fall'.

Ideally, therefore, the best engine would be one which used steam at about 1,000 °C and expanded it until its temperature had fallen to that of cold water. Unfortunately, the pressure of steam at this temperature would be enormously high and therefore it would be too dangerous to use. Carnot therefore argued that air, whose pressure does not rise so rapidly, was more promising as a working substance for a really efficient heat engine. Although this argument effectively set all previous assumptions on their heads, Carnot was entirely correct and on it the high-efficiency Diesel engine, invented at the end of the nineteenth century, was based.

Whether Carnot was *justified* in his argument was another matter. The pressures and therefore temperatures of the steam in the best engines then in use – the Cornish engine reports are invaluable for this information – indicate that the thermodynamic advantage over low pressure engines was extremely small compared with the actual improvements in efficiency that these engines achieved.[1] Carnot in short was not immediately justified in his generalisation and the majority of writers who, like Poisson, ascribed the improved performances of high-pressure engines to detailed improvements, rather than to any intrinsic factor were broadly speaking correct. But in the long run Carnot was justified in his insight; this was not, of course, the first time that a scientific advance was based on inadequate or erroneous data.

In this way the development of high efficiency steam and hydraulic engines brought about a new science as well as a

---

[1] The efficiencies of ideal engines working with steam at six and one atmospheres, or 160 °C and 100 °C respectively and with condensers at 15 °C should be 35 per cent and 23 per cent. But Cornish engines working at six atmospheres, or slightly less, had achieved increases of efficiency of two, three or even four-fold that of the best atmospheric-pressure steam engines. Evidently, this can only be accounted for by the many detailed improvements that were made at this time; the 'thermodynamic factor' being unimportant.

new technology. The technology is today manifest either in the form of Saturn rockets using heat energy to lift a given load from the earth to the moon or, more mundanely in the family of air engines which includes the Diesel engine, the gas turbine and the ubiquitous automobile engine. But, as regards the science, a further and fundamental step was required: the substitution for caloric of the concept of energy. For it was shown that in a heat engine there is not only a flow of heat from hot to cold, as Carnot rightly thought, but also a transformation of heat into mechanical energy. The refutation of the doctrine of the conservation of heat, on which the whole science had been built following Lavoisier and Laplace (1782), was followed by the establishment of the principle of the conservation of energy. And since heat is not conserved but is transformable into other forms of energy and vice versa and since the thermo-mechanical processes of nature are essentially energy transformations the concept of entropy was found necessary in order to express, in quantified terms, changes in the energy state of any particular body. This resulted in the final statement of the cosmology of heat, due to R. J. E. Clausius: the energy of the world is constant, its entropy tends always to a maximum.

Many things contributed to the mid-nineteenth-century synthesis of the doctrine of energy. In historical terms that part of the synthesis which is represented by thermodynamics is surely unintelligible without reference to the technological developments that preceded and accompanied it. The structure of Carnot's theory rested on the works of the hydraulic and steam power engineers which converged so significantly during the years 1790–1825, and in particular on the achievements of James Watt and the Cornish engineers. Even Richard Arkwright had an indirect influence on the contemporary interest in the efficiencies of various engines. The ideal Carnot engine, derived from purely technological considerations, marked the ultimate standard by which all the thermo-mechanical transformations in nature were to be measured. If therefore we still insist that the relevant science, thermodynamics, is a matter of 'pure' science alone then its origins must always remain an enigma!

5

GATEWAYS TO DEATH?
MEDICINE, HOSPITALS AND
MORTALITY, 1700-1850

by E. M. Sigsworth

Within the debate seeking to explain the causes of the increase of population in Britain during the eighteenth and early nineteenth centuries, it seems to be generally accepted that medical developments and especially the increasing provision of hospitals had, at best, no beneficial effects upon the death rate, or, at worst, a negative effect. Hospitals at this time were, as Professor Helleiner puts it, 'gateways to death'.[1] The principle foundation for this gloomy view of early hospitals remains the important article by McKeown and Brown:

> The chief indictment of hospital work at this period is not that it did no good, but that it positively did harm ... Any patient admitted to hospital faced the risk of contracting a mortal infection ... it was not until later than [the eighteenth century] that hospital patients could be reasonably certain of dying from the disease with which they were admitted, the importance of segregating infectious patients was not appreciated.[2]

Made by medical historians, such statements have commanded widespread respect amongst their economic and social brethren and have indeed become firmly embedded in the literature of economic history ... 'Hospitals were more likely to spread disease than to check it. People who went to hospital in the eighteenth century, normally died there, generally from some disease other than that with which they were admitted.'[3]

---

1 K. F. Helleiner, 'The Vital Revolution Reconsidered', *Canadian Journal of Economics and Political Science*, XXIII, no. 1 (1957), reprinted in D. V. Glass and D. E. C. Eversley (eds.), *Population in History* (London, 1965), p. 84.

2 T. McKeown and R. G. Brown, 'Medical Evidence Related to English Population Changes in the Eighteenth Century', *Population Studies* (1955-6).

3 P. Deane, *The First Industrial Revolution* (Cambridge, 1965), p. 29. See also

Did eighteenth- and early-nineteenth-century hospitals in fact deserve their reputation as 'gateways to death'?

Firstly, it is as well to look at arguments advanced by contemporaries favouring the establishment of hospitals in a period during which, between 1700 and 1800, the number of hospitals increased from two to fifty or so, with a variety of additional institutions such as dispensaries and lying-in charities.[1] Thus, for example, in 1714, John Bellers, a Quaker and an important proponent of hospital provision, published his 'Essay Towards the Improvement of Physick in Twelve Proposals By Which the Lives of Many Thousands of the Rich as well as of the Poor may be Saved Yearly'.[2] It may, at the outset, be thought odd that so optimistically entitled an essay should have contributed to the establishment of nothing more than fifty gateways to death, if such they were, but this may be no more than a particular case of a generally observable gap between good intentions and abysmal outcomes which is by no means confined to the practice of medicine. Bellers' contention was that about one-half of the deaths then occurring and similarly a great deal of sickness could be prevented by timely advice and suitable medicine, but that since, in his estimation, three-quarters of the population were too poor to procure either, then their provision should be undertaken by the State. It was his further contention that 'every able industrious labourer that is capable to have children who so untimely dies, may be accounted two hundred pounds loss to the kingdom; as for our nobility and gentry, I leave their valuation to themselves, but their Account will run very high'. From this embryonic flirtation with a primitive form of cost–benefit analysis, Bellers went on to make specific proposals including the establishment of hospitals to promote the care and recovery of the sick poor, contending that treatment could be provided in them at one-tenth of the cost of treatment in the patients' homes and that the provision of hospitals would greatly improve the training of physicians

B. Abel-Smith, *The Hospitals 1800–1948* (London, 1964), quoting McKeown and Brown to similar effect.

[1] Institutions with which, along with other specialised hospitals, this contribution will not be concerned.

[2] I am indebted to Mr J. H. Woodward, of the Institute of Social and Economic Research, University of York, for drawing my attention to this essay.

and surgeons, on the one hand halving the duration of their training and on the other enabling the medical profession to become more expert by availing itself of opportunities for specialisation which hospitals would create.

As Mr John Woodward has pointed out,[1] Bellers probably influenced the growth of the hospital system in the eighteenth century more than any other person, especially in the emphasis placed upon provision of hospital treatment for the deserving poor. As was written, for example, of the Winchester County Hospital:

> It provides for the relief and comfort of Multitudes who are unable to be at the expence of Advice or Physick, but are not distinguished by the name of The Poor, because they do not come under the care of a Parish or Workhouse, and yet are principal objects of this Charity, and most of all, entitled to the regards of the Public, since They are in present want; and are of the diligent and industrious, that is of the useful and valuable part of all Society.[2]

In York, as in other hospitals founded during the eighteenth century, the County Hospital treated 'the poor' for whose benefit the hospital was established. Patients for treatment were nominated by subscribers to the hospital's funds. Thus the subscriber of £1 per annum could have 'one out-patient on the hospital books at a time and no more'.[3] For a £2 subscription, one in- *or* one out-patient was allowed, while for £3 the subscriber could nominate one in- *and* one out-patient. Payment of a lump sum of £20 entitled the donor to the annual privileges of a person subscribing £2 yearly. This appears to have been a common arrangement in the financing of eighteenth-century hospitals. As has been written, the subscriber 'acquired prestige in the eyes of his neighbours, his employees and his tradesmen. The right of admission to a hospital was normally in his gift and he received an excellent return for his guinea. His sick servants need never be on his hands. To segregate those with contagious or otherwise

---

[1] J. H. Woodward, 'Before Bacteriology – Deaths in Hospitals', a paper given to the Yorkshire Faculty of the College of General Practitioners, Harrogate Festival of Arts and Sciences, August 1968.

[2] *An Account of the Establishment of the County Hospital at Winchester with the Proceedings of the Governors etc. from the first Institution on St. Luke's Day, 18 October, 1736, to Michaelmas, 1737*, Point 8.

York County Hospital, General Court Minutes, 28 February 1742.

unpleasant diseases was only common sense.'[1] In general, York County Hospital, in common with others, treated the sick poor thought to be deserving by a benevolent patron. In York Hospital, however, as was commonly the case elsewhere,[2] children under the age of seven were not to be admitted as in-patients 'except only those who are to be cutt for the stone'[3] and the range of other types of patient who were to be excluded varied in different hospitals. At Leeds, pregnant women, smallpox patients and those suffering from 'the Itch or other infectious Distempers' were specifically excluded from the Infirmary in 1767.[4] Shrewsbury Hospital, founded in 1747, excluded smallpox cases 'or other infectious distempers' and patients suffering from 'habitual ulcers', inoperable cancers, epilepsy, consumption and 'dropsies in the last stages'. Should patients develop smallpox whilst in the hospital they were to be removed forthwith and nursed 'in lodgings'.[5] In London, St Thomas' Hospital excluded cases with the itch, plague, scald-head or other infectious diseases or if patients were to develop such diseases once having been admitted, they were to be immediately discharged.[6] According to Woollcombe writing in the early nineteenth century, hospitals 'exclude contagious distempers as fever and smallpox in most instances and consumption in many'.[7] That patients in hospital were thus highly selected – socially to comprise the deserving poor, medically to exclude small children and women in advanced pregnancy, both categories with high mortality rates, and to exclude where possible infectious patients – must be borne in mind when considering their fates in hospital.

Hospital histories are usually fairly reticent about their

[1] W. H. McMenemy, 'The Hospital Movement of the Eighteenth Century and its Development' in F. N. L. Poynter (ed.), *The Evolution of Hospitals in Britain* (London, 1964), pp. 55–6. See also W. B. Howie, 'The Administration of an Eighteenth Century Hospital, The Royal Salop Infirmary 1747–1830', *Medical History*, v (1961), and S. T. Anning, *The General Infirmary at Leeds*, vol. I (Edinburgh, 1963), p. 81.

[2] Howie, *Administration*; Anning, *General Infirmary*; B. Abel-Smith, *The Hospitals 1800–1948* (London, 1964), p. 13.

[3] York County Hospital, General Court Minutes, 28 February 1742.

[4] Anning, *General Infirmary*, p. 81.

[5] Howie, *Administration*, pp. 50–1.

[6] F. G. Parsons, *The History of St Thomas' Hospital* (London, 1934), vol. II, pp. 207–8.

[7] W. Woollcombe, *Remarks on the Frequency of Different Diseases* (London, 1808), p. 98.

patients who, for example, appear in the massive two-volume history of the London Hospital in only six page references to 'admission of ... discipline of ... neglect of'.[1] It is a curious phenomenon, only to be comprehended perhaps by those who may have experienced the mixed sensation of anonymity combined with superfluity which can seize a hospital patient. Possibly because of the minimal role played by the patients in the published histories of hospitals, they have acquired their dismal reputation during the eighteenth and early nineteenth centuries. It is as well, however, to look more closely at the evidence upon which this reputation rests and to ask further what can be said about the fates of people who actually became hospital patients. As to the first task, McKeown and Brown base their crushing verdict upon eighteenth-century hospitals on a number of pieces of evidence. Firstly, to support the view that the importance of segregating infectious from non-infectious cases in hospitals was not appreciated, the instance is quoted of cholera patients being admitted to the general wards of St Bartholomew's Hospital in 1854.[2] Yet as has been seen, all hospitals for which rules are extant specifically sought to exclude infectious patients or if, inadvertently, they were admitted, to discharge them at once. It is, of course, one thing to make such rules, another to observe them given the severe diagnostic limitations existing during this period, but at least let it be noted that rules there undoubtedly were. Secondly, reference is made to 'contemporary accounts of the unsatisfactory conditions in eighteenth century hospitals ... in the writings of Percival, Howard, etc.' The main item here is Howard's 'Account of the Principal Lazarettes in Europe' published in 1789. Howard, a much used source, commented mainly on what he considered to be the generally poor standards of London hospitals in 1788. Outside London he visited only twelve hospitals out of a possible twenty-five and in these conditions varied greatly. Further support is adduced in a footnote reference to the effect that conditions in *British* hospitals by reference to one

[1] A. E. Clark-Kennedy, *The London: A Study in the Voluntary Hospital System*, (London, 1962).
[2] Having been inadvertently admitted to a general medical ward in 1956 suffering from poliomyelitis, the author is perhaps less impressed by this than he should be!

Parisian hospital in 1788.[1] This is particularly interesting given the comments of a subsequent writer, who, in 1808, showed that while in this hospital, the Hôtel Dieu, the mortality rate was one in five, in no English hospital did the rate exceed one in eleven patients, while in the best (i.e. least mortal) hospitals, mortality rates were as low as one in thirty-five.[2] Even in the London hospitals upon which Howard had concentrated his case and which had, deservedly, the worst reputations, the mortality rate averaged one in thirteen patients. Even this it must be observed is a long way from the 100 per cent mortality of patients which is the only statistical expression of the fashionable 'gateways to death' argument. Thirdly, there is a quotation from a book published in 1874 illustrating the high rates of mortality following surgery. Is one to infer that what was then bad was worse the further back in time one goes? Fourthly, Florence Nightingale's dictum is quoted that the first requirement of a hospital is that it should do the patient no harm, taken from the third edition of her Notes on Hospitals, published in 1863. This, of course, is one of the standard authorities for the gloomier interpretation of the role of hospitals, yet it is important to recall that despite her formidable reputation, the statistical material which Miss Nightingale produced in 1863 to show how dreadful and how mortal to the patients hospitals were, received very critical handling. Thus, the reviewer of her book on hospitals, writing in the *Medical Times and Gazette*, pointed out that she had taken the total number of deaths occuring in a hospital throughout the year and related this total to the number of patients in bed in the hospital on one particular day of the year. 'There is something audacious' the reviewer observed, 'when 24 London hospitals are accredited with a mortality per cent of inmates of 90.82.'[3] To this, Miss Nightingale did not herself reply, but she was defended in a highly emotional fashion by no less a person than William Farr. He in turn, however, went down to a crushing reply by Dr Bristowe who, with Dr Holmes, was one of the principal contributors to the *Medical Times*, both also being the authors of an important report to the Privy Council on hospitals.

1 Tenon, *Memoirs sur les hopitaux de Paris* (1788).
2 Woollcombe, *Frequency of Different Diseases*.
3 *Medical Times and Gazette*, 30 January 1864.

If, [wrote Dr Bristowe], out of a fixed population of 10,000 persons, 200 die in the course of a year, the mortality of the population will be ... 2 %. But if, during this supposed year, these same 10,000 persons had been successively inmates of an institution with 2,000 beds and the 200 deaths had happened within the walls of that institution, the result would have been a death rate of 10 %. And again, if those 10,000 persons had been inmates of an institution with 1,000 beds or one of 500 beds, the mortality would have been respectively 20 % and 40 % ... Has Dr Farr calculated the birth rate in lying-in hospitals on the same principle and attempted to draw conclusions from the results? A lying-in hospital with 10 beds habitually occupied would yield at least 120 children per annum, a birth rate of 1,200 %. The average maternal unit brings forth a litter of 12. Would Dr Farr, who assumes that his death rates of hospitals are a measure of the unhealthiness of hospitals, assume that the birth rates of lying-in hospitals are a measure of hospital air? ... Further, has Dr Farr thought of comparing the recoveries (escapes if he will) per cent in his various hospitals with the deaths per cent? A method of calculation which is good for determining the one point is of course equally valid for determining the other. The death rate (according to Dr Farr and Miss Nightingale varies from 47 to 100.5 %; the recovery rate (similarly measured) varies from 899 to 953 % ... these results might justify an enthusiast of an opposite bias in adducing the recovery rate as a proof of the admirable healthiness in the institutions which Dr Farr condemns on account of their insalubrity.[1]

To this there was no reply but, of course, it is Florence Nightingale's book which continues as a major source for the pessimistic view of hospitals.

This, then, is the evidence used to establish the current view of the negative contribution of eighteenth-century hospitals to falling mortality – little evidence drawn from that century and three references to works published during the third quarter of the nineteenth century – one relating to surgery in one hospital (to which I return below), one relating to one shortcoming in one hospital and one relating to a work of formidable repute which was thoroughly criticised by contemporaries.

That hospitals were dreadful places, that surgery was nasty and brutish, but never short from the viewpoint of the conscious patient, is doubtless true. But how dreadful were they in fact? How inimical were conditions in them to the patients' chances of survival? Did patients not only emerge from hospitals dead in the eighteenth century, but with a

[1] *Idem*, 30 April 1864.

surprised expression at being dead from some disease other than that with which they were admitted?

The records of York County Hospital are admittedly local and fragmentary, but suggest the following points:

1. That between 1740 and 1743 only 52 of the 1,708 patients treated actually died in hospital.[1]
2. Apart from those who thus died, it was *claimed* that 1,335 patients were discharged as 'cured', the balance being discharged as lunatics, incurables, fractious, self-discharged and, in one case, an imposter.
3. The precise *annual* figures for mortality in the hospital are not then available until the 1820s, but of 26,023 patients admitted between 1740 and 1783, 18,717 were claimed to have been 'cured' and 4,794 as 'relieved' (i.e. 90 per cent cured or relieved) and between 1784 and 1842, of 35,326 patients admitted, 89.5 per cent were similarly claimed to have been cured or relieved.[2]
4. When direct statistics of in-patient mortality again became available between 1825 and 1835, then in no year in this decade did the percentage of patients dying in hospital exceed 6.3[3]

It would be right to doubt the claims for 'cures' and to wonder what relief meant,[4] but the point is that, whatever happened to the patients *after* they had left the hospital, they did *not* 'normally' die in it.

There are, however, further points of interest. The first relates to the risks of mortality attending surgery. McKeown and Brown quote figures suggesting that, in University College Hospital in the quarter of a century before 1874, amputations were fatal in 30–50 per cent of cases, while for some (unspecified) types of operation mortality was as high as 90 per cent.[5] The first statistics relating directly to surgical cases in York

1 York County Hospital, *Annual Reports*, 1740–3.
2 York County Hospital, *Annual Reports*, 1784, 1842.
3 York County Hospital, *Annual Reports*, 1825–35.
4 In Edinburgh, 1729–30, it meant 'recovered so as to go about their ordinary Affairs and requiring only some Time to confirm their Health and to restore their Strength fully', *An Account of the Rise and Establishment of the Infirmary* (Edinburgh, 1730), quoted in J. D. Comrie, *History of Scottish Medicine* (London, 1932), vol. II.
5 *Ibid.* p. 120.

County Hospital are for 1868.[1] In that year, 110 operations were performed, of which 83 cases were subsequently discharged as 'cured' and four as 'relieved'; 13 were transferred to out-patients, and seven were still in the hospital at the year end. Only three died in hospital. Within this total the number of amputations was 35, of which cases only one died in hospital, 23 being discharged as 'cured', 8 being made out-patients and 3 remaining in the hospital at the year end. It may have been the case that Lister's techniques, applied in 1867, had wrought a revolution in surgical mortality in York beyond that which the great surgeon himself claimed.[2] There is no evidence that his new techniques were in fact in use there,[3] but for these surgical cases in York in 1868, as for all the available statistics for York County Hospital from 1740, one can only suggest, either that the hospital was served by successive generations of arithmetical incompetents, or chronic liars[4] – doctors, surgeons, trustees and governors engaged in a perpetual and successful

[1] York County Hospital, *Annual Report*, 1868–9.

[2] C. Singer, *A Short History of Medicine* (Oxford, 1944), p. 240. With the use of antiseptics, Lister was still experiencing a mortality rate of 15 per cent between 1867 and 1870. At Leeds Infirmary in 1861, 211 operations were performed with 16 deaths (i.e. 7.5 per cent). Between 1861 and 1874 the post-operative death rate varied between 7 and 11 per cent. At St Bartholomew's Hospital and Guy's Hospital, the death rates following operations in 1861 were 9.7 and 8.1 per cent respectively. The mortality rate following amputations in Leeds Infirmary in 1868 was 13.90 per cent. Anning, *General Infirmary* p. 40, and appendix II, p. 98. For ovariotomy operations, however, the death rate in the period 1875–77 averaged 73.2 per cent, falling thence to 6.6 per cent by the end of the century (vol. II, p. 116). Cf. also the surgical successes claimed in Dundee in 1841, n.6. In the Norwich Hospital, 910 operations were performed between 1773 and 1863 with only a 13 per cent mortality rate, though these, of course, did not *necessarily* require an incision to be made.

[3] Lister's methods are known to have been in use in Leeds in 1868 (Anning, *General Infirmary* vol. I, p. 40). It is important to remember, as Dr Anning points out, that 'the benefits of Lister's methods were probably counter-balanced by the increasing scope of surgery under anaesthetics and the danger of more extensive operations. Anaesthesia itself was a hazard at this time.'

[4] This possibility should not, of course, be wholly ignored. Mr Munro, Surgeon at Dundee Infirmary, commented in 1842 on the fact that 49 operations had been performed in the previous year without death resulting, 'some of considerable gravity' and including 24 amputations and noted: 'This has not arisen in the slightest degree from any exclusion of patients in consequence of their being incurable or otherwise unfit objects of admission, nor from any urging of patients to leave the house when they were found to be approaching a fatal termination, a mode by which a medical attendant of an hospital at any time, may bring the mortality to a convenient ratio.' H. J. C. R. Gibson, *Dundee Royal Infirmary* (1948), p. 19.

campaign to deceive an utterly gullible public, or that the hospital's records indicate that an examination of actual hospital evidence relating to the varying fates of the patients in those fifty or so hospitals established by the early nineteenth century is required before one can accept with quite that credulity which has so far been forthcoming, sweeping generalisations about the *negative* contribution of eighteenth and early nineteenth-century hospitals to falling mortality. That conditions varied considerably between hospitals is undoubtedly true, as the evidence collected by Dr Woollcombe suggests. Was York County Hospital an isolated beacon of light, shining exceptionally in the darkness which is held to have been characteristic of hospitals in the period? Woollcombe's statistics suggest not.

The second and much more difficult question raised by the fragmentary evidence for the York County Hospital relates to the dangers of cross-infection implied by the view that not only did patients die *in* hospital, but of some disease other than that with which they had been admitted. The relevant evidence relates only to the years 1740–3 for which statistics were offered relating to the various complaints from which, it was claimed, 1,335 patients had been 'cured' and begins again in 1843 with an analysis of the complaints for which patients were admitted.[1] Three points emerge from comparison of the two sets of figures. Firstly, whereas between 1740 and 1743 there had been in the hospital cases of venereal disease, none was present in the 1840s. In fact, the hospital Minutes record that such cases were barred, after 1755, 'no person having ye venereal disease shall be admitted as an in-patient'.[2] Secondly, whereas between 1740 and 1743 patients suffering from a variety of fevers, 'continual, hectical, intermittent, remittent, pleuretic' and 'worm induced, bloody flux (i.e. dysentery) and dry gripes', had been mixed indiscriminately with the rest, in the 1840s, fever cases were no longer present

[1] York County Hospital, *Annual Report*, 1843–4.
[2] York County Hospital, *General Court Minutes*, 11 February 1755. A previous attempt by the Governors to the effect that 'no unmarried person infected with ye venereal disease shall be admitted more than once to the Benefit of the Hospital', was rejected by the Trustees (*idem*, 8 November 1743). At Leeds such cases were explicitly excluded when the Infirmary was founded in 1767. (Anning, *General Infirmary*, p. 81.)

in the hospital. In fact, in March 1810, an outbreak of fever in the hospital had caused the death of five patients who had contracted the disease as in-patients, others having 'prematurely quitted the hospital thus depriving themselves of the benefits which they might have otherwise have derived'.[1] This, however, was claimed to be unusual – 'occasional instances of fevers and disorders have occurred at different former periods and, though they were not attended with such fatal effects, yet it would, on each of these occasions have been desirable to separate the infected persons from the other patients'. Already, before the outbreak of 1810, surgical and medical cases had been separated from each other.[2] Now, the hospital took steps to segregate fever cases entirely and in fact, though hampered by lack of funds, achieved this segregation by 1816.[3] The third point which is suggestive rather than substantial is that neither in the 1740s nor in the 1840s were any patients recorded as suffering from smallpox; perhaps, insofar as there had been in the 1740s, they had all died and were therefore not returned as 'cured'. Perhaps in the 1840s they were excluded anyway along with fevers generally. There is no positive evidence that they were excluded from the hospital as a minuted action of policy, as in the cases of venereal disease and 'fevers' – but does the silence of the records on this point suggest that they never *were* admitted? Three cases were discharged in the 1740s as 'infectious' – did this recognition of the dangers of infection in York extend, as elsewhere,[4] to a tacit understanding that smallpox cases were not to be admitted? Three instances with a possible fourth can be given for York County Hospital of attempts to lessen the dangers of cross-infection in the eighteenth and early nineteenth centuries. Beyond this it may never be possible to go for York, but the questions raised by this examination of the evidence – fragmentary though it is – for one provincial hospital, should be asked and may be more readily answerable for other hospitals. One may ask further, on general grounds, why was it, if hospitals deserve the reputation with which they have been endowed, that people were willing to enter them at all, and why did the

[1] York County Hospital, *General Court Minutes*, 18 December 1811.
[2] *Idem*, 13 February 1810. [3] *Idem*, 13 August 1816.
[4] See above pp. 99–100.

number of hospitals increase during the eighteenth century, and, coming back to the particular case of York and quite apart from the statistical evidence relating to mortality in the hospital there, why should it have been necessary in 1787 to pass a resolution that in-patients must be ejected after they had been resident for two months, unless there were satisfactory medical grounds for prolonging their stay?

The case in favour of falling mortality as the main cause for eighteenth- and early nineteenth-century population increase has recently been argued on the grounds that inoculation against smallpox was much more important than has hitherto been conceded.[1] The case of York County Hospital suggested that the role of hospitals as the contributors to mortality should be re-examined.[2]

At the risk of trespassing on the work of Mr John Woodward,[3] who has examined all the available surviving records of hospitals established in England during the eighteenth and early nineteenth centuries, it is possible to say that the rate of mortality of in-patients rarely exceeded ten per cent. This examination confirms the extent to which hospitals sought to exclude potentially highly mortal cases (infants, pregnant women) and cases suffering from infectious diseases. It is true, of course, that instances occurred in which patients who should have been excluded by the application of the rules were inadvertently admitted. Pregnant women, insane and epileptic patients, and sometimes cases of smallpox thus emerged in the wards of the London Hospital.[4] A woman admitted to the Radcliffe Infirmary in Oxford whose complaint was diagnosed as dropsy, astonished and in varying degrees confounded and delighted the hospital authorities by giving birth.[5] Yet it must be reiterated that the intention of the hospital rules was clear and would, in so far as it could be

[1] P. E. Razzell, 'Population Change in Eighteenth Century England. A Reinterpretation', *Economic History Review*, xviii, (August, 1965).

[2] I am most grateful to Mr T. Donaldson, the Secretary of the York County Hospital, for permission to use the Hospital's surviving records, to Dr S. T. Anning of Leeds, for helpful comments, and to Dr M. C. Barnett, of York, for permission to use the library of the York Medical Society and to Mr E. W. Cooney of York University.

[3] The remainder of this essay is substantially dependent upon his work.

[4] Clark-Kennedy, *The London*, p. 153.
Oxford Journal, 13 December 1777.

fulfilled, help to produce more favourable results for hospital treatment than are currently allowed.

Further, whilst one is haunted by stories relating the undoubted horrors of surgery – the patient conscious, or, if semi-conscious, then drunk, the surgeon performing with unsterile hands grasping unsterile instruments, wearing a frock coat stiff with the dried blood of previous patients, the whole atmosphere fraught with pain and thick with bacteria – all this must be placed in perspective when relating surgical to general hospital mortality. In fact, during the eighteenth and early nineteenth centuries, before the introduction of anaesthesia, the range of surgical operations was very limited, those performed being principally lithotomy, amputation, the setting of simple fractures, excision of cataracts, abcesses, carbuncles and cysts and trephining of the skull for depressed fractures and meningeal haemorrhage. If, as has been argued, the introduction of Davy's safety lamp increased rather than reduced mortality due to accidents in coalmines by enabling deeper and more dangerous seams to be worked, then similar effects seem likely to have followed the introduction of general anaesthesia in surgery. Surgical mortality rose overall, because, with the patient unconscious and uncomplaining, the surgeon could now attempt a wider and more drastic range of operations than hitherto.[1] Furthermore, not only did the range and severity of operations increase but the amount of surgery expressed as a proportion of total in-patients increased later in the nineteenth century. It seems likely that at least for a time, this increase, pressing harder on the physical resources of hospitals, exacerbated the dangers of sepsis (at least until after Listerian techniques became general). Thus, from the information available, it would seem that while the proportion of cases admitted into hospitals during the eighteenth century and until the mid nineteenth century rarely exceeded one in ten, the proportion in particular hospitals might have risen to one in three or even one in two by the late 1860s and early 1870s.

It is relevant here to set off also, against the *one* instance of high surgical mortality quoted by McKeown and Brown and relating to the twenty-five years preceding 1874, other instances

---

[1] The point has been made elsewhere that, without anaesthetics, the surgeon perforce must perform his task very swiftly.

than that already quoted from York County Hospital suggesting a very different outcome. Thus in the Norfolk Hospital over the whole period 1773–1863, there were performed 910 operations for lithotomy with a mortality rate of less than 13 per cent. In Birmingham General Hospital, the mortality rate for the same operation was 8.4 per cent between 1853 and 1863. At the Radcliffe Infirmary, overall surgical mortality between 1838 and 1865 was 17 per cent, that for amputations alone 13 per cent and lithotomy 14 per cent. Mortality from all operations at the Royal Berkshire was 11 per cent; that for amputations 8 per cent.

One must, of course, beware of the pitfalls which attend the interpretation of hospital mortality during this period. It was always possible for hospitals to produce statistics presenting their activities in a favourable light, especially when they depended upon voluntary subscriptions for support. It was not unknown for patients to be discharged in anticipation of their confidently forecast deaths and there were other ways of presenting mortality statistics in a more favourable light than was warranted.[1] Nor does it seem very likely that one can demonstrate finally that hospitals presented more, or less, favourable environments for their patients than would have been experienced had they remained at home, for this would require precise comparison between directly comparable groups of people in terms, for example, of age, sex, social class and nature of affliction, a comparison which the nature of eighteenth-century demographic evidence seems unlikely to permit and for this reason the contribution of hospitals to a falling death rate must remain indeterminate, though the evidence suggests that, whatever this may have been and whatever hospitals may have been like they were not, for the great majority of those who entered them as patients, 'gateways to death'.[2]

[1] Drs Bristowe and Holmes reported in 1864 that in one hospital, out of 626 patients on the register 169 were duplicates, reducing the calculated death rate from 6.5 per cent to 4.7 per cent. 6th Report of the Medical Officer of the Privy Council, London 1864, Appx. No. 15. J. S. Bristowe and T. Holmes, *The Hospitals of the United Kingdom*, p. 528.

[2] I am indebted to the editors of the *Journal of the College of General Practitioners*, Yorkshire Faculty, for permission to use in this contribution material which originally appeared in their issue for June 1966, in 'A Provincial Hospital in the Eighteenth and Early Nineteenth Centuries'.

6

RESOURCES OF SCIENCE IN VICTORIAN ENGLAND: THE ENDOWMENT OF SCIENCE MOVEMENT, 1868–1900[1]

by Roy M. MacLeod

INTRODUCTION

Among the most important developments of the nineteenth century was the gradual transformation of scientific activity from the individual, occasional pursuit of private research as an avocation, to the prosecution of science by full-time professionals. This development had implications, not only for the rate and direction of scientific research but for the social institutions, the laboratories and the scientific instrument industries upon which research increasingly relied. These in turn had profound consequences for the several thousand men of science who between 1830 and 1900 swelled the growing ranks of research in Britain.

To date, little historical work has attempted to assess or compare the extent, significance or dynamic of this development.[2] We are largely ignorant of the ways in which 'growth points' in science have been recognised or encouraged by scientists or society. We know more about the social, economic,

---

[1] Research upon which this essay draws was supported in part by a grant in science policy from the Department of Education and Science. I am grateful to the Librarians of Trinity College, Cambridge and the Royal Institution for permission to cite material in their possession, and to the Directors of John Murray Ltd, for access to selected letters concerning *The Academy*. I am also grateful to Miss E. Kay Andrews for her comments on earlier drafts.

A version of this paper has appeared as 'The Support of Victorian Science: The Endowment of Research Movement in Great Britain, 1868–1900', *Minerva*, IV (2) (April, 1971), 197–230.

[2] Notable exceptions can be found in the work of Joseph Ben-David, 'Scientific Productivity and Academic Organisation in Nineteenth-Century Medicine', *American Sociol. Review*, xxv (1960), 828–43, reprinted in B. Barber and W. Hirsch, *The Sociology of Science* (Glencoe, 1962), pp. 305–28.

cultural and political background which was vital in sustaining the particularly creative environment for scientific advance that existed in Western Europe in this period. But it has been deceptively easy to sweepingly describe such developments in broad retrospective Whiggish terms of 'professionalisation' and 'specialisation'. We are just beginning to awake to the complicated social and value adjustments taking place in Europe which governed changing relationships between the teaching, pursuit and application of physics, chemistry and biology.

At an even more concrete level, we know little about the comparative costs of research and the costs of educating scientists in different fields at different kinds of institutions in Britain and abroad at different points in time. We know little in detail about the ways in which governments, once involved in scientific choice, were obliged by political, economic or social measures, to extend or retreat from commitments, or to reserve or deploy resources. We know something about arguments systematically used to justify public spending on pure science, and the ways these arguments, owing to public apathy or pressure, have changed over time. But we know little as yet about the historical impact of such arguments on the collective consciousness of men of science. In our day, we have become accustomed to situations where scientists urge the social utility of science when asking for public money, but defend the social autonomy of science while spending it.[1] But few historians have assessed systematically the ways in which governments have used criteria of political, economic, military or professional necessity to justify the endowment of scientific education and research.

Many fruitful historical enquiries into this subject can be approached through cross-national comparisons, such as that begun several years ago by the University of Sussex and the *'Arbeitsgruppe für Wissenschaftspolitik'* at Heidelberg. These comparisons have set out to give some insight into the social and administrative experience of nineteenth-century Germany and Britain in terms of such factors as differential rates of scientific growth in different fields and universities; changes in the cost patterns of research and administration; changes

---

[1] This is well illustrated in the recent *mémoire de crise* of Sir Bernard Lovell, *The Story of Jodrell Bank* (London, 1965).

in the composition of fields, in the social backgrounds and occupational expectations of scientists; trends in the development of degrees, periodicals and communication networks; and patterns in governmental support of science and technology under competing national and international political and military pressures. Any such comparisons must naturally involve the study of social and scientific attitudes towards science within the broader context of social and political circumstance.

The present essay is intended to illustrate the development of such attitudes in the context of one particularly critical phase of Victorian reform which had far-reaching significance for the social status and support of research in this country. This development can best be described as it was by contemporaries, in terms of the movement for the 'Endowment of Research'.

This movement of ideas gathered strength between 1860 and 1875 and is especially important for three reasons. For the first time, though not for the last, it persuaded the nation that pure research was basic to material prosperity. It convinced the public that pure research in Britain was in decline and could only be increased by public or private support endowing a new class of researchers. Finally, it contributed to the gathering wave of reforms in the universities and the introduction of science into the Civil Service.

Between 1830 and 1850, following the outcry of the 'Declinist' faction, led by Charles Babbage and Sir David Brewster, a small shower of honours, pensions and awards had descended upon science, and the Government had looked with favour on many new scientific expeditions and enterprises. In 1849, following the exertions of the British Association and the reforms within the Royal Society, a parliamentary grant of £1,000 was given to be administered by the Royal Society for the promotion of original research. But these efforts were insufficient for two reasons. First, the nature of scientific research, particularly in the physical sciences, had changed; apparatus and experiments were no longer within the reach of individual men. As William Crookes observed in 1876:

The facts and truths that lay near at hand have already been gathered in. We have now to go farther afield, to use costlier, because rarer, materials, to correct the approximate determinations of our predecessors, and in so doing to employ expensive instruments of precision. Little could be done in these days with apparatus such as that used by Dalton or by Davy at the outset of his career. Hence it has become more difficult for a poor man, unaided, to win his way to eminence.[1]

The parliamentary grant helped the amateur scientist by defraying some of his out-of-pocket expenses. But it could not suffice for the 'poor man unaided' who was becoming far more visible in the community of research. By the middle of the nineteenth century, science, particularly in England, had begun to lose its implicit and traditional association with the leisured aristocracy. A rising 'middle-class' of science, educated not at Oxbridge, but at medical schools, in London, or in Germany, was coming into existence. In 1850 it was quite small – of the order of a few hundreds – but by 1875 it had begun to reach into the thousands. Membership of the thirteen chief metropolitan scientific societies rapidly doubled from about 5,000 in 1850 to about 10,000 in 1870 and thereafter increased to 20,000 by 1910.[2] Not all of these people wished to do research as a career. But those who did were often unable to do research without some form of external subsidy. These looked to the State for action and to the universities for security. For numbers of middle-class or lower-class men of science such empirical expressions of Royal patronage as the Civil List, the Royal Medals and the small Royal Society grants were merely tokens of sublime aristocratic assurance that research never conflicted with the pursuit of daily bread. Alas, the facts suggested otherwise.

Unlike the 'Declinist Movement' of the previous generation, the movement for the Endowment of Science which began in the 1860s and 1870s reflected the determination of men of science and learning to seek not personal honours, or even honours for science, but living wages for themselves and their fellows. Developing well after Chartism had faded and in an age of growing material prosperity, this appeal was not dissimilar to attempts at reform begun by other professional

1 [W. Crookes], 'The Endowment of Scientific Research', *Quarterly Journal of Science*, VI (October 1876), (n.s.) 485.
2 R. M. MacLeod and E. K. Andrews, *Selected Science Statistics relating to Research Endowment and Higher Education, 1850–1914* (Mimeograph, Science Policy Research Unit, Sussex University, 1967).

associations in the period. There was little, if any, revolutionary sentiment in these protests; indeed, strong dissatisfaction with existing arrangements for the encouragement of fundamental research went closely with a strong belief that these arrangements were perfectible. The appeals of men of science also reflected a growing appreciation of the value of research and possibly a more sophisticated patriotism than the 'Declinists' of 1830, sensitive to military and commercial rivalry with France, had displayed.

By the 1850s, in any case, German example had begun to dictate academic standards. Far from the strong anti-continental spirit of the 1820s, the Endowment of Research movement was not defensively chauvinistic; if anything, it suggested instead a certain collective 'anti-patriotism' and a reluctance to follow continental practices in stressing the relationship between scientific distinction and national glory. Science was becoming an inward-looking, self-interested vocation. Its practitioners were looking for the kind of social acceptance which implied not merely passive toleration but active support. In making their case, they cited the advantages of utility and prestige to be gained from science, but they no longer made the expansive early Victorian claims that understanding would inevitably bring 'improvement'. They wanted support, but not interference, and would make no promises of quick success. Science was growing, and growing for its own sake; fundamental research had its own virtues alongside applied science, medicine, and the commercial exploitation of nature.

Against this background, the movement for the Endowment of Research began. By 1900, it had helped fulfil the dreams of scientific men seeking government support, and had thrown light on the new role of the ancient universities in stimulating both research and teaching. In passing it had revealed the ambivalence of late-Victorian society towards research, and illuminated the tug-of-war between academic, administrative and parliamentary opinion that has become part of our contemporary experience.

I. UNIVERSITY REFORM

Support for the endowment of research first caught public

attention by its association with an increasing wave of proposals between 1850 and 1868 for the reconstruction of British education generally and higher education at Oxford and Cambridge in particular. Dramatic portents were seen in university affairs. Perhaps it was not quite true, as one contemporary observed, 'if any Oxford man had gone to sleep in 1846 and had woke up again in 1850 he would have found himself in a totally new world'.[1] But these years unquestionably saw significant changes in 'Old Tory' Oxford. Following the defection of Newman to Rome, the Tractarian movement had for the moment collapsed, and theology had quietly acquired a Germanic nuance in Oxford common rooms. Moreover, fifteen years after the attacks of Sir William Hamilton and the *Edinburgh Review* the 'one man – all subjects' method of teaching was on the decline, and in its place had come talk of university reforms, German philosophy and the superior virtues of the professorial system.[2] Old values were no longer above question. In the wake of Lyell's geology, a scientific spirit was abroad in the land. As Mark Pattison later observed, it was to this 'silent permeative genius of science that the growth of a large and comprehensive view of the function of a University and the desire to discharge it spread among Oxford liberals'.[3]

In 1850 Oxford introduced Honours Schools in Modern History and the Natural Sciences. The same year, the Liberal ministry of Lord John Russell responded to a memorial from the Royal Society by appointing Royal Commissions to enquire into the finances and duties of both ancient universities. Not all university men reacted kindly. 'I understand that Lord John's announcement of the University Enquiry Commission took all parties by surprise', wrote George Airy to William Whewell, Master of Trinity. Whewell himself, as a Peelite Conservative, was annoyed; during the late 1840s, he, together with Babbage, Peacock and Herschel, had worked out plans for reforming the teaching of science at Cambridge. In 1848, shortly after the election of Prince Albert as

[1] Mark Pattison, *Memoirs* (London, 1885), p. 24.
[2] Cf. Lewis Campbell, *The Nationalisation of the Old English Universities* (London, 1901), p. 14.
[3] Quoted in *ibid.* p. 305.

Chancellor, Cambridge had introduced the Moral Sciences in the first new tripos created since the Mathematical and Classical Triposes began (in 1747 and 1824 respectively). But these reforms were tempered by Whewell's determination that no new tripos should threaten the academic supremacy of mathematics. Even Peel, who had appointed Whewell to Trinity, angrily exclaimed to Prince Albert:

The Doctor's assumption that *a century should pass* before new discoveries in science are admitted into the course of academical instruction, exceeds in absurdity anything which the bitterest enemy of University Education would have imputed to its advocates. Are the students at Cambridge to hear nothing of electricity?[1]

To the University Commissioners, however, Oxford, rather than Cambridge, was the chief target. It was Oxford, slumbering under the shrouds of theological texts,[2] that had caught the fury of Lyell's attacks in 1845, and that had prompted Brewster's sweeping criticisms of university science. 'I am convinced', Airy predicted, 'that Cambridge generally will come well out of it ...',[3] and so Cambridge did. The Cambridge Commissioners paid tribute to Whewell's reforms. But they also observed that the progress of 'that great innovator, "Time", and the "operation of social causes little within her control" had kept the University from attaining "her true position" and had seen her "become imperfectly adapted to the present wants of the country so as to stand in need of external help to bring about some useful reforms".' The Commissioners laid particular stress on the absence of instruction in civil engineering and modern languages, and urged greater emphasis on university instruction outside the colleges. Private coaches like E. J. Routh and William Hopkins had often groomed men merely to pass examinations. Hopkins himself admitted to the Commission that the Mathematics Tripos rendered difficult 'the perception of the

---

[1] J. G. Crowther, *Statesmen of Science* (London, 1965), p. 184.
[2] See Charles Lyell, *Travels to North America* (London, 1845), and for a discussion of the religious question at Oxford and Cambridge see V. H. H. Green, *Religion In Oxford and Cambridge* (London, 1964), and A. I. Tillyard, *A History of University Reform* (Cambridge, 1913).
[3] *Whewell Papers* (Trinity College, Cambridge), A.1.80. Airy to Whewell, 4 May 1850.

logical connection of one part of a subject with another'. The Commission concluded that better official instruction could make Humboldts of those gentlemen-students who spent their university years devising 'mean and fruitless ways in which wealth may be squandered and leisure abused'. In 1851, reforms quickened by the Commission led to the creation of the Natural Sciences Tripos, and eventually to scientific instruction on a regular basis.

Following the two Commissions, an Oxford University Act was passed in 1854 which abolished the Test for matriculation and the BA, and provided for Executive Commissioners to reform the expenditures of the colleges and the government of the university. The analogous Act for Cambridge in 1856 freed matriculation and Bachelors' degrees from the Test.[1] Both Acts opened the universities to greater numbers of dissenters and opened fellowships to merit, and in so doing improved opportunities for scientific men.

During the late 1850s, the ancient universities came under increasing public pressure to reform their methods. 'Efficiency' in the public services, transfigured by the Northcote–Trevelyan reforms and the scheme of open competition, accelerated the adoption of stiffer standards in university and school examinations. But these reforms met repeated obstacles. In 1851, some jealous colleges had refused to reveal their wealth to the Royal Commissioners, and had declined to reduce fellowships to endow chairs. There were also frequent protests from Oxford and Cambridge dons against the imposition of the German professorial system. One protest took the form of an Aristophanic parody:

> Professors we, from over the sea,
> From the Land where Professors in plenty be,
> And we thrive and flourish, as well we may,
> In the Land that produced one Kant with a *K*,
> And many Cants with a *C*.[2]

Under such circumstances, the rate of change was glacial.

By the mid-1860s, the extent to which necessary reforms had

---

[1] The BA degree, however, did not carry a vote in the Senate. The MA degree and college fellowships remained subject to the Tests, however, until 1871. Campbell, *Nationalisation*, p. 127.
[2] Quoted in Campbell, *Nationalisation*, p. 81f.

been delayed was widely recognised. But Palmerston's Government, preoccupied by foreign policy questions, found little time for domestic reforms. Between 1865 and 1868, however, a number of events in quick succession crystallised public and parliamentary opinion. In 1864 the Clarendon Commission reported in favour of some increase in the proportion of time given to natural science in the great public schools;[1] within the next three years, new movements for technical education, for reform in the Science and Art Department syllabus, and for increased numbers of science teachers all gathered strength.[2] 'At what a rate the chariot of Democracy is driving', Professor Jowett of Balliol wrote in June, 1867, 'It almost takes away one's breath.'[3] In 1867 a Select Committee on Oxford testified vigorously to the neglect of new learning in the university.[4] In the same year, British manufacturers gave a disappointing performance in the industrial section of the Paris International Exhibition, and Lyon Playfair and the Taunton Commission put the blame on inadequate British secondary education.[5] Finally, in 1868, two books – Mathew Arnold's *Schools and Universities on the Continent* and a volume of *Suggestions on Academical Organisation* by Mark Pattison, Rector of Lincoln College, Oxford – appeared. Arnold demonstrated in his investigations on the continent in 1867 the disadvantages under which Britain laboured in the diffusion of scientific knowledge. Pattison's suggestions struck deep at the political roots of opposition to university reform.

In the 1850s, the consequences of the University Acts had been to improve the efficiency of universities as examining

[1] *Report of the Royal Commission on Certain Public Schools* (The Clarendon Commission) (1864) xxi. See especially evidence given by Lyell, Faraday, Hooker, and Airy in November 1862.

[2] *Report of the Select Committee on Provision for Instruction in Theoretical and Applied Sciences to the Industrial Classes* (1867–8), (432). xv.1. See also the Standing Committee of the Royal Society of Arts on Technical Education, created in January 1867, which reported in July 1868. *J. Soc. Arts*, xiv (31 January 1868), 183–209; xvi (24 July 1868), 627–42. See also George Gore, 'On Practical Scientific Instruction', *Q.J. Sci.* vii (1870), 215–29.

[3] Campbell, *Nationalisation*, p. 152.

[4] Campbell, *Nationalisation*, p. 140.

[5] *Report Relative to Technical Education of the Schools Inquiry Commission* (the Taunton Commission), xxvi (1867), p. 267.

machines, and to strengthen the colleges as 'endowed boarding schools for adults'.[1] But Pattison attempted to show how the system of Honours Schools, caught up in the pressure of competitive examinations, had lost sight of its wider educational purposes. Moreover, Oxford, by abandoning the pursuit of new knowledge for its own sake, had failed to set the pace of higher education for the country. Pattison's own experience of Oxford life had led him from the 'Collegiate Ideal', which he had commended to the Royal Commission of 1850, to the opposite ideal of a university governed by the progress of research and learning. Backed by the Liberal wing of the university whose ranks were swelled by the opponents of clericism and veterans of the *Essays and Reviews* controversy, Pattison argued carefully that research was vital if the university wished to ensure properly balanced scholarship.

In order to make Oxford a seat of education, it must first be made a seat of science and learning. All attempts to stimulate its *teaching* activity, without adding to its solid possession of the field of science, will only feed the unwholesome system of examination which is now undermining the educational value of the work we do.[2]

Goldwin Smith disagreed with Pattison and disapproved of any attempt by the government to assume responsibility for university research; on the contrary he advised that,

the expenditure of *public* money [my italics] in sinecures for the benefit of persons professedly devoted to learning science has been decisively condemned by experience ... the best way in which the university can promote learning and advance science is by allowing its teachers, and especially the holders of its great Professorial chairs, a liberal margin for private study ... [3]

To some, the distinction between teaching and research seemed trivial. Lewis Campbell, Professor of Greek at St Andrews (and later Honorary Fellow of Balliol), likened it to asking whether the highest end of individual life is beneficial action or the cultivation of virtue.[4] But it was clear that movements for university reform, whilst revising the teaching

[1] J. S. Cotton, 'The Intentions of Founders of Fellowships' in Mark Pattison *et al. The Endowment of Research* (London, 1876), p. 30.

[2] Mark Pattison, *Suggestions on Academical Organisation* (London, 1868), p. 198.

[3] Goldwin Smith, *Reorganisation of the University of Oxford* (1868), pp. 23–4.

[4] L. Campbell, 'The End of Liberal Education', *Address to Students at St Andrews* (Edinburgh, 1868), p. 5.

system, had also impelled the universities away from that reverence for learning which had characterised their earliest foundations.

II. THE MID-VICTORIAN SCIENTIFIC WORLD

Outside the ancient universities, a group of 'new men', equipped with German research training, or exhilarated by the popularity of science, rose to prominence in science. One particularly important group emerged in London around T. H. Huxley, John Tyndall, Lyon Playfair, John Lubbock, Edward Frankland and Norman Lockyer. By the 1860s these men had found themselves in commanding positions in the small world of Victorian science. Nine of them came informally together in the famous 'X-Club', which began to reach into the daily affairs of the Royal Society, the British Association, the Science and Art Department, and scientific publishing.[1] One of the nine had given evidence before the Clarendon Commission in 1862; two were members of the Taunton Commission in 1865 and two were elected to the Society of Arts Committee on Technical Education in 1868. Whatever differences divided them socially and economically, they seemed to share at least three premises – a sound respect for the importance of research, a belief that Britain, however well she had distinguished herself in the Great Exhibition of 1851, lacked a sound foundation of scientific education and research, and a belief that State or private action to meet these objects was of the utmost importance. First in the literary weeklies of the day, then in the *Quarterly Journal of Science*, and finally in the country's leading scientific paper – *Nature* (founded by Lockyer in 1869) – their views became known throughout the English-speaking world.

Members of this small circle differed in many respects from both the 'cultivators of science' who had rallied round David Brewster and Vernon Harcourt at the British Association in 1831, and from the gentlemen and scholars who comprised the Royal Society in the early 1850s. The new reformers were still self-taught in science, though a few derived from scientific

[1] R. MacLeod, 'The X-Club: A Scientific Network in Late-Victorian England', *Notes and Records of the Royal Society*, xxiv (December 1970), 305–22.

families and three of the club had German doctorates. None had degrees from either Oxford or Cambridge. Like the 'Declinists', they had little patience with Oxbridge intransigence; unlike the 'Declinists' they were much more aware of scientific life outside Britain, much more familiar with the research methods and educational systems of continental Europe, and much more concerned with the serious cultivation and diffusion of new knowledge in society.

The motives of this band of friends were often influenced by years of personal financial uncertainty in the pursuit of science, strengthened by a growing conviction that science was necessary and worth public reward. Unlike Faraday, who was even then cited as a paragon of indifference to wealth and comfort,[1] most would-be researchers without private means were convinced that the question of a scientific career was at root a financial one. Economic incentives certainly played their part in Huxley's constant flow of publications, his charity to the Scientific Relief Fund and his close personal interest in scientific salaries. The ancient universities gave little hope for new appointments, with few exceptions, while existing chairs in science had become life-long sinecures. In London, University College, with its strong scientific tradition, offered very limited prospects for research. In 1854, Thomas Hirst resigned his chair at University College giving the explanation that:

I cannot at present do any original work, [and] it is only by devoting myself wholly to lecturing that I can keep up my number of students at the College, and thus secure my bread. [...] as my strength fails my prospects will necessarily be worse at U.C.; these facts I say decided me at length to apply for an appointment of an inferior order, perhaps, but of a less inglorious and more remunerative character. Moreover, if I succeed, I shall come in contact with good and influential men and myself be able to influence to some extent the character of education in England.[2]

---

[1] Faraday's salary at the Royal Institution was £200. After his retirement, he received a pension of £300 from the Government, which gave him what we would consider a middle-class income. But Faraday deliberately avoided contractual agreements which would have brought him greater wealth, lest they also distract him from research. 'I cannot afford to become rich', he allegedly once said. This sentiment was widely cited. See [George Gore], 'The National Importance of Scientific Research', *Westminster Review*, XLIII (1873), 358.

[2] *Hirst Diaries* (Royal Institution), IV, f.28, February 1859.

Outside the universities, things were worse. A. H. Garrod, a physician turned physiologist and sub-editor of *Nature*, mocked the future of a scientific career as,

little more than a phantom. The prospects of a post in any Government institution, such as the British Museum, is, to say the most, scarcely a pittance, and there are many of the best workers who would undergo many privations rather than have to devote the greater part of their lives to the drudgery of an educational appointment.[1]

To a scientific man of no means outside the universities, the alternatives, broadly speaking, were three: to teach in the schools, to leave the country, or to protest. It is likely that Britain 'lost' scores of men to the colonies and the United States. Huxley, Tyndall and Playfair would probably have emigrated to Australia or North America during the 1840s had not posts in private establishments on government instructions – in Playfair's case wrought by the personal intervention of Sir Robert Peel and the Prince Consort – arisen at the last moment. The Government was employing scientists in increasing numbers, but there was no attempt to create posts in a systematic fashion. In the event, government agencies were unable to provide a career structure for scientific research.

In the late 1860s the London network, building on their experience in the British Association Committee of 1855, began to arouse political interest in science. Their plans were quickened by a little-known elderly ex-Indian army officer and amateur astronomer, Lt-Col. Alexander Strange.[2]

In August 1868, Strange delivered a paper 'on the Necessity for State Intervention to Secure the Progress of Physical Science' to the Mathematics and Physics Section of the British Associ-

---

[1] *Nature*, IX (29 January 1874), 237.

[2] Alexander Strange (1818–76), educated Harrow, served in Indian Army as cavalry officer and later Inspector of Scientific Instruments for the astronomical and geodetic sections of the trigonometric survey of India. He retired to England in 1861 and served as a member of the Council of the R.A.S. 1863–7, and as Foreign Secretary, 1868–73; he was elected to the Royal Society in 1864 (the same year the X-Club was created), and served on its Council, 1867–9. His Indian experience made him adamant about the accuracy of measuring instruments, and the part they played in physical research. See *The Academy* (25 March 1876), 290; J. G. Crowther, *Statesmen of Science* (London, 1965), pp. 237–69.

ation meeting in Norwich. The paper aroused immediate attention. Strange, with Playfair, had recently been a juror at the Paris Exhibition. When Playfair returned to begin his struggle for technical education, Strange looked instead to the support of fundamental research. In his paper, he appealed to the spirit of one of the British Association's earliest objectives: to remove any disadvantage of a public kind which impeded the progress of science.[1]

There was no doubt in Strange's mind that State participation was vital to research. He took for granted that any abstract question whether scientific investigation should be aided or even carried on by Government had already been settled by the irresistible verdict of circumstances. As Strange observed in the *Quarterly Journal of Science*, science instruction could not prosper at the universities until students wanted to learn science; and students could not turn to science until there was hope of a career.[2] At Magdalen, Oxford, a demy-ship in science once went begging, because, as the best candidate asked, 'What am I to do for a living, after I have completed my studies?'[3]

Following the Norwich meeting, the British Association, in November 1868, appointed a committee of twelve, which included Tyndall, Frankland, Thomas Hirst, Huxley – essentially the 'X-Club' – plus Playfair and Lockyer. The Committee was asked to determine whether there was sufficient provision for the vigorous prosecution of physical science in Britain. In March 1869, the committee issued a circular to several men of science, asking:

1. Whether any course could be adopted to improve their field, whether by Government or by private initiative.
2. Whether there were grounds for asking for such initiative, and
3. Whether the interests of the community were 'sufficiently involved in the more vigorous development of scientific

---

[1] 'On the Necessity for State Intervention to Secure the Progress of Physical Science', Address to the Maths and Physics Section, *Report of the British Association* (1868).

[2] [W. Crookes], 'On the Teaching of Natural Science at the Universities', *Q.J. Sci.* VI (October 1969), 500.

[3] *Ibid.* p. 500.

knowledge' to warrant the employment of state aid, either

(a) through the creation of new institutes for experimental and observational research,

(b) the extension of old institutions, or

(c) the enlargement of grants to individuals for apparatus and materials.

Several months later, the Committee reported its conclusion that, judged by any responsible standards, there was insufficient national provision for research. Hitherto research had paid the community 'but it had not paid the man'.[1] The community advantage wrought by research implied an obligation of support on behalf of the community itself. This obligation would not be satisfied merely by the establishment of a scientific observatory, by sponsoring physical measurements, creating one or two museums and providing out-of-pocket expenses for talented amateurs, but by allocating reasonable sums of money to individuals prepared to pursue a full-time vocation in scientific research.

Many in the British Association shared the Committee's view, but others feared State interference. *Nature*, for example, published a letter from Alfred Russell Wallace, protesting against what *Nature* called the 'Science Reform movement' because 'Experience shows that public competition ensures a greater supply of the materials and a greater demand for the products of science and art, and is thus a greater stimulus to true and healthy progress than any Government patronage.'[2]

On the other hand, there seemed grounds for arguing that 'where the State has a finger there will be patronage, and the preference of inferior agents who have the support of friendly recommendations, to superior agents who are standing alone'.[3] Already, in any case, the State was spending £140,000 a year on Museums, Gardens and Surveys, while the Science and Art Department Estimate for 1869–70 was over £225,000.[4] More important, however, was the categorical belief, evident especially among university men, that research should not be

---

[1] [W. Crookes], 'On National Institutions for Practical Scientific Research', *Q.J. Sci.* VI (January 1869), 48.

[2] 'Government Aid to Science', *Nature*, I (13 January 1870), 279–88.

[3] *Q.J. Sci.* VI (January 1869), 48–9.　　[4] See *Nature*, I (7 April 1870), 589–90.

divorced from instruction, and the corollary that research could bě properly endowed only through the universities. Jowett, for example, argued that there was no opposition between original research and a moderate amount of teaching.[1]

Even where reformers agreed that state support was needed, they differed about how this should be distributed. On balance, those most enthusiastic for state intervention and 'Science Reform' had little experience of university life and were not Oxford or Cambridge men. This was particularly evident among the 'X-club' and its concentric networks. On the other hand, strong arguments in favour of linking teaching with research came chiefly from the universities. In his inaugural lecture at University College, London, in October, 1869, Professor A. W. Williamson delivered 'A Plea for Pure Science' and insisted that research should not be allowed to develop outside the context of education. Henry Roscoe whose spacious laboratories at Owens College, Manchester, were among the best in England, urged that scientific research, was, through the teaching of scientific method, the best training for everyday commercial life;[2] and, James Clerk Maxwell, in his inaugural lecture at Cambridge in October 1871, in a laboratory made possible by private benefaction, stressed the advantages of doing research in the university with the resources available there.[3] At Oxford, Sir Benjamin Brodie wished to found new research institutions within the universities, with staff closely connected to university teaching. In London, on the other hand, Huxley and Lockyer were strongly in favour of independent support for research, however much this research might in practice contribute to university teaching.[4]

Whatever the best connection between teaching and research might be, the case for support was sufficiently clear to the British Association and the Government. In February 1870, Gladstone's administration agreed to appoint a Royal Com-

[1] Campbell, *Nationalisation*, p. 190.
[2] H. Roscoe, 'Original Research as a Means of Education', Address at the Opening of Owen's College, *Nature*, VIII (23 October 1873), 538ff.
[3] J. Clerk Maxwell, *Introductory Lecture on Experimental Physics* (London, 1871).
[4] *Nature* pointed out that almost all continental researchers taught as well, and that even 'in this country the greater number of our most distinguished men of science are professors and teachers'. 'The Royal Commission on Science', *Nature*, I (10 February 1870), 375. See also *The Academy*, III (1 December 1872), 460.

mission under William Cavendish, seventh Duke of Devonshire, to study national provision for scientific instruction and the advancement of science.[1] The Duke, a distant relative of Henry Cavendish, the chemist, had taken the Tripos as revised by Babbage in 1829. In 1861, he had succeeded the Prince Consort as Chancellor of Cambridge and had since actively followed the reform movement there.

The Secretary of the Devonshire Commission was the ubiquitous Norman Lockyer. Two others (Sharpey and Miller) had been active in building research schools at University College. One (Samuelson) had served on both the Acland Committee in 1867 and the Society of Arts Committee on Technical Education in 1868. Two of its nine members (Huxley and Lubbock) were members of the 'X-Club'.

The Commission sat for six years, met 85 times, interviewed over 150 witnesses and published eight reports and four massive volumes of evidence. Although instructed to look particularly at scientific instruction in schools, museums and universities, it soon raised searching questions about the state of British science as a whole and research in particular.[2] Some reports were more conclusive than others; some virtually assumed the truth of what they set out to prove. The first report, which appeared in March 1871, examined the institutions concentrated in South Kensington, and recommended that the Government combine the Royal School of Mines and the Royal College of Chemistry into a single science school with a single staff of professors in mathematics, physics, chemistry and biology.[3] The second report, issued in March 1872, confined itself to technical education and to endorsing improvements in the policies of the Science and Art Department which had long been sponsored by the London network. The third report, dealing with Oxford and Cambridge, appeared in August 1873; the fourth, on national

---

[1] The Commission included the Marquis of Lansdowne; Sir John Lubbock; James Kay-Shuttleworth, MD; Bernard Samuelson, MP; W. A. Miller (London); H. J. S. Smith (Oxford); William Sharpey (London); George Stokes (Cambridge); T. H. Huxley (London). Historical commentaries on the Commission can be found in D. S. L. Cardwell, *The Organisation of Science in England: A Retrospect* (London, 1957), pp. 92–8, and in Crowther, *Statesmen of Science* (London, 1965), pp. 222–33.

[2] *Nature*, IV (17 August 1871), 302.

[3] The first brief report was printed in full in *Nature*, III (30 March 1871), 421.

museums, in January 1874; the fifth, on provincial university colleges, in August 1874; and the sixth, seventh and eighth, on schools, the Scottish universities and government provision for science, appeared in June 1875.

Over these four years, editorial comments in *Nature* and the literary quarterlies kept public interest in the Commission alive. The Commission revealed much evidence of large government expenditure on what could be considered 'scientific' research, justified on grounds of prospective naval or commercial rewards; indeed, as the history of the Arctic and *Challenger* expeditions demonstrated, this definition could be interpreted widely. Moreover, the Government had increased its expenditure on science-related activities dramatically since the 1850s.[1] It was, in fact, doing a good deal, but it was not *seen* to be doing so, and much science that was supported was hampered by lack of co-ordination or narrow notions of departmental control. This absence of strategic thinking, and the implied waste of scientific resources, was the chief line taken by the 'Science Reformers' who repeated in public views which they had expressed officially to the Commission. In 1870, 1871[2] and again in 1872, Alexander Strange demanded that scientists should have rewards and standing comparable to the practitioners of any other learned vocation.

It has hitherto been too much of the custom, [he said] to treat men of science as exceptions to all other professions; to assume that whilst it is quite proper to enrich and ennoble soldiers who fight for pay, lawyers who evade or apply the law according to circumstances, physicians who kill or cure as seemeth best to them, and even divines, whose missions to save souls might be deemed a sufficient privilege ... [the man of science] should work for love, and die, ... in poverty.[3]

It seemed plausible that, in the interpretation of nature, no less than in the interpretation of religion, the labourer should

[1] Cf. 'Government and Scientific Investigation', *Spectator*, XLIV (22 July 1871) 882–4; cf. also: Anon. *Correspondence between the Royal Geographical Society and the Government* (London, 1873).

[2] Cf. *Journal Soc. Arts*, XVIII (1870), reported in 'The Relation of the State to Science', *Nature*, I (7 April 1870), 589–91.

[3] 'On the Necessity for a Permanent Commission on State Scientific Questions', *J. Royal United Service Institution*, xv (1870), 537–66, reprinted in *Nature*, IV (15 June 1871), 133; 'On Government Action in Science', *Report to the Mathematics and Physics Section of the British Association* (1871), p. 56.

be worthy of his hire. W. B. Carpenter, the physiologist, dwelt on England's peculiar need:

If England was behind Germany in original investigations, it was not, as is sometimes said, because Englishmen are inferior to Germans in ideal power, but because the German universities are so arranged as to afford a career to men who choose to devote their lives to study. In England such men, having no means of making a livelihood by the pursuit of science, are obliged to turn their attention to a 'practical profession'.[1]

Through the early 1870s, the distressed state of scientific men was recounted again and again. 'It is known to all the world', lamented *Nature*, 'that science is all but dead in England.' By this was meant not the 'Jury' science of exhibitions and practical technology, but 'that searching after knowledge which is its own reward'.[2] 'Whether we confess it or not', Lockyer wrote, 'England so far as the advancement of knowledge goes, is but a third or fourth rate power.'[3] From the start, the solution was evident. 'It is the question of "scientific careers" that is the pressing one, and the one most difficult to settle', one correspondent agreed.[4]

These appeals for State assistance were seconded by George Gore, an industrial chemist who had privately set up his own Institute for Scientific Research in Birmingham. Gore was no university man, and had neither wealth, title, nor professional degree. He earned his living by chemical analyses, a notoriously precarious livelihood, and soon found his way into the reform party. 'Scientific discovery and research', he told the Social Science Association at Plymouth in 1872, 'is national work and it is the duty of the State to provide and pay for it.' The justification was to him obvious:

because the results of it are of immense value and indispensable to the nation; also because nearly the whole benefit of it goes to the nation, and scarcely any to the discoverer, and because there exists no other means by which scientific investigators can be paid for their labour.[5]

In April 1873, Gore appeared in the *Westminster Review* condemning the 'great multitude of rich manufacturers,

---

[1] *The Academy* (1 December 1872), 460.
[2] 'A Voice from Cambridge', *Nature*, VIII (8 May 1873), 21.
[3] 'Our National Industries', *Nature*, VI (6 June 1872), 97.
[4] *Nature*, II (12 May 1870), 25.
[5] G. Gore, 'On The Present Position of Science in relation to the British Government', *Transactions of the Social Science Association* (Plymouth, 1872), 280.

merchants, capitalists and landowners who had profited from research without ever contributing to its support'. William Flower, the biologist, declared in a letter to *Nature*, in July 1873, 'If scientific men are reluctant to speak out on such topics for themselves, the lovers of science among men of influence, wealth and position are the more bound to speak for them.'[1] In the absence of private or industrial munificence either to independent research, universities or scientific societies, the state was the only possible patron. Without help, Gore believed, physical and chemical research in Britain would disappear.

The 1870s seemed particularly anxious for chemistry; Faraday, Graham, Mathieson and Miller had died, leaving no obvious heirs. The number of British articles in the *Journal of the Chemical Society* and *Chemical News* was dwindling. Young men were being turned away from research and lost to the professions. The evidence of Edward Frankland before the Devonshire Commission showed that Germany was producing four and a half times as many investigators in chemistry and six times as many scientific papers each year, including half the number that appeared in British journals. Similar conclusions were drawn for physics, biology and geology.[2] William Crookes and other reformers rejected the possibility that Germans were superior in ideas, but acknowledged their greater research facilities. Although Britain's industrial revolution had preceded Germany's by sixty to eighty years, Germany's 'research revolution' of the 1840s and 1850s had

---

[1] *Nature*, VIII (24 July 1873), 244.
[2] *Devonshire Commission Mins. Evid.* 1874, p. xxiii 35. Frankland's estimates were among the few attempts to quantify and compare the British position; his assertions were accepted unquestioningly by several authors. See Gore, 'The Promotion of Scientific Research', *Fortnightly Review*, XIV (ns) (1873), 510–11; [G. Gore], 'The National Importance of Scientific Research', *Westminster Review*, LXIII (ns) (1873), 353. Charles Appleton, 'Economic Aspect of the Endowment of Research', *Fortnightly Review*, XVI (ns) (1874), 522–3, also reprinted with additions as 'The Endowment of Research as a Form of Productive Expenditure', in M. Pattison, *et al. Essays on the Endowment of Research* (London, 1876). See also [Crookes], 'The Encouragement of Scientific Research', *Q.J. Sci.* VI (ns) (1876), 468; Crookes, 'England's Intellectual Position', *Journal of Science*, I (3rd series) (1879), 521; and Cardwell, *Organisation of Science*, p. 96. See also [B. C. Brodie], 'Scientific Research and University Endowments', *Nature*, VIII (12 December 1872), 97. On physiological botany, see 'Obstacles to Scientific Research', *Nature*, XI (26 November 1875), 62.

been creating a challenge for the last twenty to twenty-five years.

English chemists at least had the advantage of a commercial career, but there was little of direct relevance to business in physics, and nothing in biology. One professor of biology reportedly advised his pupils to give up their study and enter chemistry as 'there was no pursuit of a career for them in anything else'.[1] There were government posts, like those in government observatories, offering opportunities for research; but these were generally not open to young researchers. 'They are not indeed, necessarily awarded to science workers at all', wrote Richard Proctor, 'nor when so held, have they invariably been found to encourage steady work in science.'[2] 'Indeed, it would seem almost as though election to those well paid offices had been the sole end and aim of work ... so thoroughly has original research ceased, or become unfruitful, when the desired post has been secured.'[3] For Gore, however, the 'most satisfactory way of rewarding scientific discoverers and serving national interests at the same time' would be the creation of salaried state professorships for original research.[4]

Gore's suggestion quickly won support. Francis Galton in *English Men of Science*, published in 1874, agreed that action was necessary. 'Science has hitherto been at a disadvantage ... in enlisting the attention of the best intellects',[5] Galton warned. Only financial inducements, operating through State sponsored posts in Government and the universities, would provide the answer.

III. THE ENDOWMENT OF RESEARCH MOVEMENT

While advocates of direct state intervention marched past the Devonshire Commission, advocates of less State action and more local initiative gathered in Oxford. In 1872, just after the second report of the Devonshire Commission, but before the

[1] Charles Appleton, 'Economic Aspect of the Endowment of Research', *Fortnightly Review*, XVI (ns) (1874), 524, quoted in Richard Proctor, 'The Endowment of Scientific Research', reprinted in the *Popular Science Monthly*, VII (1875), 362.
[2] Proctor, *Endowment*, p. 357. [3] *Ibid.* p. 358.
[4] Gore *op. cit.* p. 360.
[5] Francis Galton, *English Men of Science* (London, 1874), p. 258.

Commission had moved to Oxford and Cambridge, another Royal Commission was appointed to enquire into college finances at Oxford and Cambridge. In November the same year, a group of about twenty Oxford liberals, reformers and men of science, most of them strongly influenced by continental fashions in historical, theological and scientific research, met at the Freemasons Tavern in London. From this meeting grew the Association for the Study of Academical Organisation, established to consider 'the low state of learning and science in the two older Universities'.[1] Charles Appleton, editor of *The Academy* and Fellow of St John's College Oxford, believed that the struggle begun by Pattison had far to go.[2] Appleton, a man consumed by enthusiasm for order, preached the German spirit of idealism and *Wissenschaft* to the dry congregation of Oxford dons. He coined, or at least put a new meaning to, the phrase 'the endowment of research'.[3]

The reformers' first meeting in London resolved that whatever the Universities Commission decided:

> The chief end to be kept in view in any redistribution of the revenues of Oxford and Cambridge is the adequate maintenance of mature study and scientific research, as well for their own sakes, as with the view of bringing the higher education within the reach of all who are desirous of profiting by it.[4]

Appleton devoted himself to the cause of redistributing college revenues to research and abolishing competitive exams until his death in 1879. What *Nature* was to tell the world of science, the *Academy* would preach in the world of letters.

The reformers' resolution, signed by about seventy men, led directly to discussions about the nature of research, the

---

[1] Cf. Diderik Roll-Hansen, 'The Academy, 1869-79: Victorian Intellectuals in Revolt', *Anglistica*, VIII (1957), 77. The Association was given leader space in an article by Brodie in *Nature*, VII (12 December 1872), 97–8.

[2] Charles Edward Appleton (1841–79), classical philologist, man of letters, and vigorous reformer in Oxford University politics and international copyright law. See John H. Appleton and A. H. Sayce, *Dr Appleton; His Life and Literary Relics* (London, 1881).

[3] H. A. Bruce, Home Secretary in Gladstone's first administration and formally responsible for the Devonshire Commission, believed the phrase was invented by Mark Pattison (see H. A. Bruce, *Life of Lord Aberdare* (Oxford, 1902), vol. II, p. 255), though Pattison himself attributed it to Appleton. (*The Academy*, 19 February 1881, 127.)

[4] *The Academy* (1 December 1872), 459.

abolition of Prize Fellowships, the need for more professors, the improvement of teaching and the introduction of new branches of study. In the meantime, the Universities Commission issued its report. Its revelations confirmed the reformers' case. Lyon Playfair told the House of Commons in May 1873 that, while the Scottish universities taught a man how to make a thousand a year, the English universities merely taught him how to spend it. Annual revenues of £170,000 were allegedly spent in educating about 2,000 although only half of those actually sought honours degrees. Vast sums supported fellowships, but between 1850 and 1870, only 12 of a total of 200 fellowships at Oxford colleges had been awarded in science. At Cambridge, three fourths of all university prizes in 1869 and one-half of all college prizes in that year, were awarded in English and Classics. The Sedgwick Prize was the only prize available in the natural sciences. After 18 years, the Natural Sciences Tripos had still not begun to attract wide interest. Between 1861 and 1870, 95 students passed the honours examination, fourteen of whom would become Fellows, but the annual increase was very slow. In 1869, 73 men were placed in the Classics Tripos, 111 in Mathematics, but only 13 in Natural Science.[1] In 1870, there were only six science chairs (excluding medicine) at Cambridge, and two of those were still associated closely with medicine. Only one (zoology) was of recent creation (1866). Among the colleges, Trinity had one science lecturer, Sidney Sussex had one and St John's had two. Downing had two, but both were shared with medicine.[2]

The Association had several meetings and won wide support in both universities. In May 1873, a memorial was drafted by a group of Cambridge dons urging the abolition of life fellowships, and more efficient provision for teaching and private study. At Lockyer's request, J. S. Cotton wrote for *Nature* a series of six unsigned articles advocating the endowment of research and calling attention to the importance of direct

[1] See *Nature*, civ (6 November 1919), 256. It must be said that the Natural Sciences Tripos was not made an independent avenue to an honours degree until 1861. Cf. Arthur Gray, *Cambridge University: An Episodical History* (Cambridge, 1926), p. 289.
[2] T. G. Bonney, on 'Natural Science at the University of Cambridge', *Nature*, 1 (3 March 1870), 451–2.

state aid through a national scheme of research fellow-ships.[1]

But soon differences appeared, both among those who con-trolled college endowments and among those who were dis-turbed 'by being called upon to learn before [they] taught'.[2] Pattison preferred not to abolish fellowships or fellowship exams, but to convert the fellowship into a body whose work ranged from full-time teaching to full-time research. John Stuart Mill preferred to keep the fellowship system and closely connect teaching with research.[3] Such personal differences denied the group a united front. Moreover, there were arguments with the 'practical' scientists, represented by Roscoe and Gore, who took a more utilitarian line and who disliked the Association's élitist assumptions. Henry Roscoe declaimed in the *Spectator* against Pattison's apparent desire for 'us in England to look up to Oxford as the great representative of every kind of intellectual activity',[4] while Appleton came back against the 'shallow money-grubbing spirit of the commercial classes', [e.g. the industrial scientists of Manchester and Birming-ham].[5]

Hostility towards the movement soon developed. *Punch* caricatured the Oxford movement as one of 'research for endowment', and as one colleague later recalled, the name of researcher was invented especially to stigmatise the holders of Appleton's 'unpalatable' doctrine. To decry Appleton became a popular pastime: 'If you wish to please the dominant party in common rooms, it was only necessary to sneer at research and researchers.'[6] The Association had a second meeting, chaired by Sir Benjamin Brodie, but, in Pattison's words, it attempted only to propagate an idea. It died in late 1873, having tried to do nothing more.

In August 1873, however, the publication of the Devonshire

---

1 'The Endowment of Research', *Nature*, VIII (26 June 1873), 157–8; (10 July 1873), 197–8; (24 July 1873), 237–8; (31 July 1873), 257–8; (14 August 1873), 317–8; (11 September 1873) 377–8.
2 *The Athenaeum* (1 November 1873), 563.
3 *The Academy* (19 November 1881), 127.
4 *Spectator* (30 November 1872), 1521.
5 Appleton in *The Times* (31 December 1874).
6 Appleton and Sayce, *Dr Appleton*, p. 81. The editorial conflict between Murray and Appleton is illuminated by correspondence kindly made available to me by the present John Murray, Junior.

Commission's third report on Oxford and Cambridge gave Appleton fresh hope. This report examined the courses and examinations in science, the system of tutorial instruction, the relation of the universities to technical and professional education, the scientific institutions within the universities, and the supposed duties of the universities towards the advancement of science. On balance, the Commission felt that the collegiate tutorial system should be preserved, but complemented by new university chairs. The continental professorial system had been tried since 1852, but because college tutors had virtual control of university examinations, professors were sometimes unable to attract students to unexamined courses. The Devonshire Commission reported that, partly because of this examination system, science teaching and research training had not greatly improved. More university chairs, supported by funds contributed by the colleges, and closely linked with college life through tutorial stipends and pensions, were the only satisfactory means of improvement. For Oxford, the Commission recommended two chairs in physics, two in chemistry, one in mathematical physics, one in applied mechanics and engineering and five new chairs in biology and medicine.[1] Citing the model research laboratory and classes of Sir William Thomson at Glasgow, the Commission stated that the first duty of new professors was to advance knowledge. The Commission also recommended reforms in the university museums, and the institution of a doctorate in science, along German lines.

These recommendations for new chairs and degrees did not completely satisfy the 'researchers'. The chief task at Oxbridge was to move science into the colleges. In 1871, the net income of Oxford colleges amounted to £300,000, of which £91,545 was paid in fellowships. The Commission had recommended the creation of fellowships in natural science. Cambridge did not reveal its total income, but reported that college fellowships annually cost £92,820 at £200–£300 apiece, normally terminable only at death or marriage. These

---

[1] In oral evidence, Mark Pattison said twenty to thirty science chairs were needed at Oxford, and others stressed the great need for skilled assistants, demonstrators and university lecturers. Cf. 'The Report of the Science Commission on the Old Universities', *Nature*, VIII (21 August 1873), 317, 337–41.

were the chief endowments which could be diverted towards research. To assist younger men to enter science 'free from pecuniary anxiety', the Commission therefore urged the universities to create senior and junior classes within the fellowship and to allow a strong bias among the juniors towards research.

These far-reaching recommendations were fundamental to the reconstruction of academic life in England over the next half century. Gradually more scientific men began to flow to the universities. In 1872, the Board of Studies of the Natural Science School at Oxford attempted to improve the science syllabus, placing emphasis on wide general knowledge of science.[1] In June 1874, the Cavendish laboratory at Cambridge was formally opened, and *Nature* gamely prophesied that 'the genius possessed by Professor Clerk Maxwell and the fact that it is open to all students of the University of Cambridge for researches will, if we mistake not, make this before long a building very noteworthy in English science'.[2] But the traditional relationship between colleges and their universities could not be quickly transformed. Indeed, not until a change in statutes in 1882 were Cambridge colleges taxed for the purposes of the university.[3]

In the meantime, the 'endowment of research' movement struggled for acceptance. Reviewing the third report of the Devonshire Commission in *Nature*, J. S. Cotton (later Appleton's successor at the *Academy*) referred to the 'absurdity' of the fact that:

the lack of pecuniary means can be the main difficulty which has hitherto in the richest country in the world, hindered original investigation in the sciences. The natural harvest of scientific discoveries which England might annually reap, has ... been checked by the irregularity with which the labourers have been rewarded and the comparative indignity with which they have been treated. For a certain class of scientific investigators of a strikingly practical character, the public will always be willing to sanction large Parliamentary grants; but for the permanent Endowment of Research and the continuous support in a worthy position of the researchers, not

[1] But see M. Foster's critical review, 'The Oxford Scheme of Natural Science', *Nature*, VI (23 May 1872), 57–8.
[2] 'The New Physical Laboratory at the University of Cambridge', *Nature*, X (25 June 1874), 139.
[3] Gray, *Cambridge University*, p. 303.

MEN IN POSSESSION.

Plate 5 'With a possible view to further appropriation, the Ministers instituted an inquiry into the possessions and sources of revenue of the several Universities'. (From *Judy*, 17th January 1872).

only the aid of the nation at large, but the wealth and prestige of our ancient universities are required.[1]

In October 1874, the Universities Commission reported, and Cotton, again reviewing for *Nature*, concluded that 'University education could be made self-supporting'.[2] If the colleges would not redistribute their wealth internally, they could be compelled to do so by law. But this required parliamentary action of extreme delicacy. In any event, the Government itself seemed best qualified to be the systematic benefactor. The Commission's Minutes of Evidence were published in May 1874, and won fresh support.[3] In the meantime, the Devonshire Commission's fourth report appeared, testifying that only two universities in Britain (Edinburgh and London), actually offered degrees in science,[4] and demonstrating wide discrepancies in faculty salaries. The fifth report showed that Owens College (Manchester) and University College (London), as well as the other university colleges united by the examination system of London University, were unable to expand their science faculties in the absence of outside help. Industry, with few exceptions, had shown little interest. City and merchant guilds were often generous, but unpredictable, sponsors. Private philanthropy in support of scientific research was nowhere to be seen. Government aid, both in capital and maintenance grants, was the only real alternative.

Following the fifth report and the report of the University Commissioners, Appleton renewed his campaign in the *Fortnightly Review* and the *Pall Mall Gazette*.[5] Finally, in the *Spectator* of 24 October 1874, he published a 'Draft Scheme for the Endowment of Research' which remains a historic attempt to define organised research as a systematic requirement of a modern university. Appleton admitted that he knew little of the environmental conditions which affected scientific dis-

---

[1] [Cotton], 'The Endowment of Research: v', *Nature*, VIII (14 August 1873), 297.

[2] J. S. Cotton, 'The Endowment of Research: v, *Nature*, VIII (14 August 1873), 297; (14 May 1874), 21–3; 'The Universities Commission Report', *Nature*, x (15 October 1874), 475–6; (22 October 1874), 495–6.

[3] *Nature*, x (14 May 1874), 21–3.

[4] *Seventh Report of the Devonshire Commission* (1875), XXVIII, pp. 3, 6 (hereafter cited as the Devonshire Commission).

[5] Cf. *Fortnightly Review*, XIV (ns) (October 1874), 1.

covery, and recommended this subject to Galton; the chief purpose of his scheme was simply to 'prevent the waste of that capacity where it does happen to exist by being diverted into those various practical channels of activity in which men without private means are accustomed to get a living'.[1] According to Appleton's scheme, young graduates would, upon recommendation by their tutors or professors, and perhaps by competitive examination, be chosen for support by a distinguished Board of Electors, to do specific pieces of research for very limited periods.

Appleton's plan set out to secure for a few 'citizens of the Republic of Science' payment equal to, but not greater than, the average income they would receive in a legal, medical or diplomatic career – though, he added reflectively, 'enough to live upon, ... perhaps not enough to marry on'. If the candidate showed evidence of succeeding in his research by the end of his tenure, as indicated by acceptance by the Royal Society or other learned bodies, his 'precarious and terminable' grant would be renewed for periods amounting in the end to 10 or 12 years, at a salary rising to the income of a 'barrister, or a medical man in fairly good practice, or a clerk who had been a dozen years in a public office, or of a junior partner in an average business – say, £800 to £1,000 a year'. If he won fame, he would be eligible for an annuity on an equally liberal scale.

To complete his scheme, Appleton suggested that the learned societies should be endowed sufficiently to carry on the business of assessment, to publish transactions, and generally to help men of science set high standards of scholarship. This endowment would also rescue the societies from being forced to admit 'from sheer want of funds ... a multitide of persons who have no pretension to the character of *savants*'.[2]

Once again, the source of this endowment was the burning question. *Nature* reported its 'surprise' that Appleton's scheme had been so well received. 'The evening organ of the Conservative party' in a sentence 'which could not have been

---

[1] *Spectator* (24 October 1874), 1329–30, reviewed in *Nature*, XI (5 November 1874), 2.

[2] *Ibid*. p. 1330.

written a bare twelvemonth ago', remarked that 'The general principle of the need of some sort of endowment for science is generally admitted, and in the main features of the scheme there is much to recommend it to a prudent public.'[1]

In June 1875 appeared the sixth, seventh and eighth reports of the Devonshire Commission. From the civil estimates of 1869–70 the Government spent, at most, £400,000 on scientific museums, expeditions, learned societies and the scientific work of central departments. The Commission accepted that the 'progress of Scientific Research must in a great degree depend upon the aid of Government. As a nation we ought to take our share of the current scientific work of the world.'[2] Accordingly, they followed the recommendations of Strange and *Nature* that the Government create a Ministry of Science and Education, with a council of scientific advisers; that the scientific facilities of civil departments be augmented and that a national technical laboratory and physical observatory be built.[3] The Commission embraced the recommendations of the scientists; 'it would be their own fault', J. S. Cotton observed, 'if they let the issues remain any longer in the domain of theory'.[4] Over the next 50 years, most of these recommendations were realised in some form. Each was highly significant to the constitutional development of scientific administration. But none was of more ultimate significance to the conduct of basic research than the Commission's recommendations to increase the Parliamentary Grant of the Royal Society and to give direct and stipendiary personal grants to individual men of science.

---

[1] [J. S. Cotton], 'The Prospects of the Endowment of Research', *Nature*, xi (5 November 1874), 1–2.

[2] *Eighth Report of the Devonshire Commission*, p. 2. Both reports were abstracted at length in *Nature*, xii (12 August 1875), 285–8; (19 August 1875), 305–8; (2 September 1875), 361–3; (9 September 1875), 389–92; (30 September 1875), 469–70. The seventh report, dealing with the universities of London, Scotland, Trinity College, Dublin and Queen's University, Ireland, was reported in *Nature*, xiii (11 November 1875), 21–2.

[3] *Eighth Report*, p. 47. See Strange's letter to *The Times* (6 February 1874); see also, 'A Minister for Science', *Nature*, ix (12 February 1874), 277. A proposed Science Council of 30 members was outlined by Strange, anonymously, in *Nature*, xii (16 September 1875), 431.

[4] *The Academy* (4 September 1875), 252.

Roy M. MacLeod

IV. THE FRUITS OF PROTEST

1. *Personal stipends for research*

Between 1875 and 1880 the movement reached its climax. During the life of the Devonshire Commission, Gladstone's Government had taken little interest in 'science reform'.[1] However, with the accession of Disraeli's second administration in 1875, the reformers' prospects brightened. Derby and Salisbury, both members of Disraeli's new Cabinet, had both given evidence before the Commission, strongly urging government participation in science. The question of 'patronage' involved in the issue of personal stipends vexed the Liberals' conscience, but left Derby and Salisbury, themselves amateur scientists of long standing, quite unperturbed. In January 1875, Salisbury had praised Owens College and acknowledged the claims of science to a role in higher education.[2] Scientific men were seen as vital to the national interest. 'Who knows how many discoveries might be worked out', Derby asked Edinburgh students in his Rectorial address in December 1875,

> how many conquests of man over Nature secured if, for, I do not say a numerous body, but even for some 50 or 100 picked men, such modest provision were made that they might be set apart, free from other cares, for the double duty of advancing and diffusing science . . . Whatever is done, or whoever does it, I think more liberal assistance in the prosecution of original scientific research is one of the recognised wants of our time.[3]

In a reply to his question in parliament about the Devonshire Commission in February 1876, Lyon Playfair was told that the new administration was considering what action it should take.[4] In early March, Playfair, with Sir John Hawkshaw,

---

[1] Gladstone's aversion to science was well known. W. E. H. Lecky admitted there were 'wide tracts of knowledge with which he [Gladstone] had no sympathy. The whole great field of modern scientific discovery was out of his range.' Cf. Lecky, *Democracy and Liberty* (London, 1896), p. xxxi. Lord Morley recalled that Gladstone watched science 'vaguely and with misgiving . . . from any full or serious examination of the scientific movement he stood aside, safe and steadfast within the citadel of Tradition', John Morley, *Life of Gladstone*, (London, 1905), vol. I, p. 209.

[2] Cf. Balfour Stewart [of Owens College] 'The Marquis of Salisbury on Scientific Education', *Nature*, xi (28 January 1875), 241.

[3] Address to Students at Edinburgh, reported in *Nature*, xiii (23 December 1875), 141.

[4] Hansard, *Parliamentary Debates* (Third Series), p. 227 c.551 (21 February 1876).

President of the British Association, led two deputations to the Government to induce them to act on the Devonshire recommendations. In reply, the deputation was told that the third report (on Oxford and Cambridge), was in the hands of Lord Salisbury, while the Government had taken steps to set up a solar physics laboratory in South Kensington. The Government, Playfair was assured, was 'quite alive to the importance of the subject'.[1] That said, the scientific reform issue shifted from the public forum to the council chambers and became a matter of administrative arrangement.

In the spring of 1876 the question of increasing aid to scientific research was discussed by the Duke of Richmond and Gordon (Lord President of the Council), Sir Stafford Northcote (Chancellor of the Exchequer), and W. H. Smith (Financial Secretary to the Treasury). The Treasury agreed to sanction a vote for research, including provision for personal payments, to appear in the estimates of the Science and Art Department.

The decision to give the Science and Art Department control of the vote was hotly contested by Ralph Lingen (Permanent Secretary of the Treasury) and a strong supporter of Gladstonian finance. Lingen deplored the explosive growth of the Department and the soaring costs associated with scientific education. He feared that, without direct Treasury control, research would lead inevitably to unchecked and unproductive spending. He also felt that the role of the state in relation to scientific research was being misconstrued. 'I cannot see', he wrote, 'what is the obligation of Government while the Royal Commissions are sitting on two universities with more than £700,000 per annum to dispose of.'[2]

Following conversations in April and May 1876, between the President of the Royal Society, the Treasury, the Lord President of the Council, and Lord Sandon (Vice President), it was agreed that the Society would keep control of its original £1,000 grant-in-aid but that a new fund of £4,000 would be created and administered by the Science and Art Department on recommendations of a special Committee of the Royal

[1] 'Scientific Instruction and the Advancement of Science', *Nature*, XIII (9 March 1876), 371.
[2] T1/7522B/6048/1876, Minute, R. Lingen to W. H. Smith, 12 April 1876.

Society. The Science and Art fund could be used for personal stipends, as well as for research expenses.[1]

Although accepted by the Government, the Treasury viewed the new personal stipends with great reluctance. Lingen opposed the policy of instituting salary payments 'where now nothing but assistance towards the cost of experiments ... is afforded', because it 'opens the door to a sort of expenditure doubtful both in kind and degree'.[2] Only the intervention of W. H. Smith (Financial Secretary) backed by the Cabinet's opinion succeeded in quashing Lingen's objections.

But doubts were not confined to the Treasury. Even among the London network there were differences. 'It is well known', Lockyer darkly warned, 'that there are many Fellows of the Royal Society whose positions as workers in science need not be too clearly defined who view with mistrust the liberality of the Government.'[3] Two years earlier, Sir Joseph Hooker had said that Government should help provide 'appliances, and buildings and colleges' but that private initiative alone should 'find the workers and funds when they require it for their support'.[4] Now, in December 1876, Hooker wrote to Darwin in a similar vein:

> Government may do much, but it must always be under such vexatious restrictions that it tries a man's temper and patience, let his patriotism be what it will, to undertake the expenditure of what Government gives, and I fear it must ever be so. Between ourselves, I think there will be a wretched outcome of the Government Fund (the £4,000 p.a.). I am sure that if I had uncontrolled selection of persons to grant it to and was free to use my authority over them, I could have got ten times more done with the money. I shirked the subject in my address.[5]

The subject was heatedly discussed at the 'X-Club' later in December. Tyndall, who had himself endowed in the USA

[1] T1/7522B/9795/1876, Minute, W. H. Smith, 1 July 1876. *Minutes of the Government Grant Committee* (hereafter abbreviated as *Mins. GGC*), 18 May 1876, Richmond and Gordon to PRS, 29 April 1876. The official correspondence was loyally reprinted for all to see in 'Government Aid to Scientific Research', *Nature*, XIV (29 June 1876), 185–6.

[2] T1/7522B/6048, Lingen to W. H. Smith, 12 April 1876.

[3] 'Government Grants in Aid of Science', *Nature*, xv (1 March 1877), 369.

[4] L. Huxley, *Life and Letters of Sir Joseph Dalton Hooker* (London, 1918), vol. II, p. 231, Hooker to Darwin, 22 December 1876.

[5] *Ibid.* p. 235.

research fellowships in physics with the $14,000 he earned during his lecture tour in 1872,[1] ruefully predicted that 'a good deal of heart burning is likely to flow from this gift. It is not one into the need of which we [the Royal Society] have fairly and naturally grown, so that it will have to be managed instead of healthily assimilated.'[2] Professor George Stokes asked whether the personal grants would go to mature scholars or to 'young men of promise'. If the former, the Society would open itself to criticism for giving money to men who were already reasonably comfortable. If the latter, on what basis would the selection be made? If candidates were required to submit written work, who would referee it? Could the Committee members, who received no fees or travelling expenses, be asked to do so? If testimonials were to be taken up and if interviews were to be held, wouldn't these place a premium on personality and personal acquaintance?[3]

These were, however, procedural questions on which the Fellows agreed to take a chance. The Royal Society, reluctant executor of the Government's benefaction, went ahead as proposed. At the end of December 1876, the new Government Fund Committee (GFC) was launched on a five-year trial run, and was invited:

1. to initiate or carry on investigations and to provide private funds for their being carried out, whether by conferring grants on competent persons, or by offering prizes for the solution of problems;
2. to consider applications from persons desirous of undertaking investigations;
3. to apply funds for computation and formation of Tables of Constants and other laborious and unremunerative scientific work.[4]

Claims from different fields of science would be considered

---

[1] One was at Harvard, one at Columbia, and one at the University of Pennsylvania. See 'Endowment for Scientific Research and Publication', *Nature*, LI (13 December 1894), 164–5.

[2] *Tyndall Papers* (Royal Institution), vol. XI, f.644, Tyndall to Thomas Hirst, 17 December, 1876.

[3] *Stokes Papers* (Cambridge University Library), 'Proposals' (1877).

[4] Minutes of the Government Fund Committee (hereafter abbreviated *Mins. GFC*) 7 December 1876.

by three specialist Committees of Recommendations and reviewed by a General Purposes Committee. Personal grants were to be limited to twelve months' tenure and annual reports were required. Three members of the 'X-Club', two members of the Devonshire Commission and several signatories to Appleton's resolution were among the twenty-six members of the new Committee. *Nature* hailed it as inaugurating 'a new era in the scientific activity of our country'.[1]

Almost immediately, however, the award of personal grants to individual researchers and research assistance to university professors intensified the growing tendencies towards specialisation and separation between scientists in government service and academic life. The Government's policy, in fact, set up a competition for funds. In 1880, William Flower, Owen's progressive successor at the Royal College of Surgeons and future director of the Natural History Museum, declined to serve on the Royal Society Committee on grounds that government money was being dissipated in the support of amateurs at a time when many professional men in the nation's museums were labouring under unsatisfactory conditions. Flower also objected, however, to the encouragement of 'cottage research' and the demoralisation of individual scientific men by a programme which made their lives too easy. The programme seemed, in his view, too much like outdoor relief:

The large increase of this method of subsidising science, accompanied as it is with the (as it appears to me) humiliating necessity of personal application in each case, must do much to lower the dignity of recipients and detract from the independent position which scientific men ought to occupy in this country.[2]

While the Royal Society programme selected for academic rather than for government scientists, it was by no means clear that the Royal Society, or the Government, had weighed the long-term consequences of its action. William Spottiswoode, treasurer of the Society, admitted that, in principle, it was desirable to permit men without sufficient means to do research they could not otherwise afford. On the other hand, it was questionable whether the Society should assume moral

[1] 'The Endowment of Research', *Nature*, xvi (14 June 1877), 117.
[2] *Mins. GFC* (19 February 1880); William Flower to Huxley, 27 January 1880.

responsibility for encouraging men 'not yet of independent income' to interrupt 'the business of their life' merely for the sake of science.[1]

Of course, no one knew exactly how many would-be men of science were not doing research because they could not afford the time. But this question at least was answered by March 1877 when ninety-eight applications for grants totalling nearly £14,500 were received by the GFC. In the end only thirty-three of these projects were approved,[2] but it was clear that a pool of potential researchers definitely existed. The growing popularity of the grants became worrying when William Thomson (later Lord Kelvin) and William Crookes, both members of the GFC, announced their intention of resigning from the Committee in order to apply for grants themselves. Their threatened departure could have deprived the Government of the services of men of science 'on whose judgment and knowledge the country would place the greatest reliance'.[3] But fears for the integrity of the scheme soon disappeared. Those wishing research assistance simply left the GFC until their grant-aided projects were completed.

In reviewing the scheme in 1881 the Committee said that if the scientific value of the work was not easily measured, the £20,000 spent between 1877 and 1881 had given rise to twenty-one articles in the *Philosophical Transactions* and 150 articles in the Proceedings and Journals of other scientific societies.[4] Many researches were also still in progress. During the first five years 417 applications had been received, beginning in 1878 with 181. After 1878, the numbers fell to 103 and later to 72, but the successful applications increased from 18 per cent in 1878 to 58 per cent in 1881. The GFC assured the Department that the declining number of applications reflected a reduction in 'useless and unsuitable schemes' rather than

---

[1] *Mins. GFC* (11 January 1877). To help explain the differences between the existing forms of Government support, Norman Lockyer devoted a leading article in *Nature* of March 1 1877 to 'Government Grants in Aid of Science'.

[2] The records do not reveal the criteria selection, but Hooker confirmed that no successful application requested more than £400. Presidential Address to the Royal Society, 30 November 1877, *Proc. Roy. Soc.* xxvi (1877), 432.

[3] *Mins. GFC* (15 February 1877), Norman MacLeod, Science and Art Department to Secretary, Royal Society, 29 January 1877.

[4] *Report of the GFC* (1881).

reduced interest in the plan. Applications through the 1880s and 1890s varied between 40 and 80 a year with a rejection rate varying between 30 per cent and 50 per cent. Between 1850 and 1914 the grant assisted 938 men in 2,316 projects, with sums amounting to nearly £180,000. By 1910, however, applications had risen to over 100 a year, and within the fixed allocation, grants were reduced to trifling sums of more horrific than economic significance. By then, however, the significance of the grant had begun to decline. In 1851, it had constituted about 50 per cent of all parliamentary funds in annual aid of science. By 1860, however, it had declined to 16 per cent and by 1900 to 5 per cent of all State expenditure on science as the Government's commitment to scientific activity grew steadily.

11. *The* Essays *and the Universities*

The development of the endowment campaign was carefully followed abroad. Shortly after President Gilman of Johns Hopkins University visited Europe in 1875, he created ten new fellowships in philology, literature, history, ethics, political science, mathematics, engineering, physics, chemistry and natural history. The object of these fellowships was explicitly to give 'scholars of promise the opportunity to prosecute further studies, under favourable circumstances, and likewise to open a career for those who propose to follow the pursuit of literature or science'. Johns Hopkins, in Gilman's view, would be benefited 'by their presence and influence, and by their occasional services' no less than by the prospect of acquiring new junior staff.[1]

In Britain, few such generous benefactions appeared.[2] From their return to power in 1874, however, the Conservatives began to take a political interest in university reform. In the 1850s, most Tories had opposed government interference in the universities, largely on the grounds that university reform had become synonymous with the admission of Dissenters.[3] After

---

[1] *The Academy* (17 June 1876), 585.
[2] Cf. The new research fund for the Chemical Society, begun by gifts from T. Hyde Hills and G. D. Longstaff, *Nature*, xiii (13 April 1876), 461.
[3] Campbell, *Nationalisation*, p. 80.

1876, however, this was no longer an issue. To Appleton's great joy, in February 1876, Salisbury, then Chancellor of Oxford, introduced the Oxford Reform Bill in the House of Lords. Salisbury's views coincided with Derby's, and both were prepared to restore to the university her ancient pre-eminence over the colleges. Professorships and new buildings would be supplied from forfeited 'idle fellowships'. 'We are of the opinion', he said,

that the mere duty of communicating knowledge to others does not fulfill all the functions of a University and that the best Universities in former times have been those in which the instructors, in addition to imparting learning, were engaged in adding new stores to the already acquired accumulation of knowledge.[1]

In recent times, research had repeatedly suffered because 'it had been pursued by men who have not possessed arms sufficiently robust to enable them to fight their way'. With the abolition of Tests at Oxford and Cambridge in 1871, the nonconformist sector from which many scientists had traditionally come,[2] could at last enter university life. 'The teachers at Oxford are not clergymen now' said Salisbury, 'and ... we want to get them from other sources than that which formerly supplied them'. With reform, the ancient universities would give arms to research.

The parliamentary campaign, which *Nature* called the 'first fruits' of the Devonshire Commission, was also the climax of Appleton's efforts.[3] In May 1876, Appleton published through Henry S. King, an edited volume of ten *Essays on the Endowment of Research*. Six essays were by other Oxford men, including Mark Pattison, Henry Nettleship (Corpus), T. K. Cheyne (Balliol), J. S. Cotton (former Fellow of Queen's) and S. H. Sayce, Professor of Comparative Philology, H. C. Sorby, Professor of Geology at Sheffield and W. T. Thiselton Dyer, Assistant Director of Kew Gardens.[4] The book had a tremen-

[1] *Hansard*, Parliamentary Debates (House of Lords), Third Series (24 February 1876) 227, cols. 791–803.
[2] Cf. Nicholas Hans, *New Trends in Education in the Eighteenth Century* (London, 1951).
[3] J. S. Cotton, 'The Government Scheme of University Reform', *Nature*, XIII (2 March 1876), 341.
[4] The Essays included Mark Pattison's 'Review of the Situation'; J. S. Cotton on 'The Intentions of the Founders of Fellowships'; Appleton on 'The Economic

dous impact, and was reviewed in nearly every major literary journal in England.[1]

The movement for the Endowment of Research [said the *Spectator*] is no longer the impracticable crusade which it appeared to be twelve months ago. The activity of its promoters and the unexpected sympathy which it has inspired in official quarters, has enabled it to make its way into the arena of practical politics.[2]

The World was even more explicit. 'In the speech in which he introduced the Oxford Reform Bill, Lord Salisbury made himself the mouthpiece of the *Essays*.'[3]

The *Essays* illustrated the broad spectrum of opinion held among university men on the question of research. Appleton continued to view research not in terms of natural science, but in terms of *Wissenschaft*; Pattison, for reasons peculiar to Oxford, saw the problem as one of medieval privilege resisting modern scholarship. Sorby spoke for the privately supported amateur who had done well financially on his own and who wanted to patronise science himself, while Thiselton Dyer, the biologist, represented the 'civil scientists' who saw the importance of pure research to public well-being in such fields as cellular biology and nutrition. Utilitarian research, for example in navigational astronomy and geology, was well and good, but it was also necessary that the State 'without a *present* utilitarian stimulus, should set apart some portion of its income for the systematic attack of problems, the solution of which may be reasonably expected, but which are beyond the scope of teaching establishments'.[4]

The *Essays* seized public opinion already anxious about

Character of Subsidies to Education'; Appleton again on 'The Endowment of Research as a Form of Productive Expenditure'; Sayce on 'The Results of the Examination System at Oxford'; Sorby on 'Unencumbered Research: A Personal Experience'; Cheyne on 'The Maintenance of the Study of the Bible'; Sayce again on 'The Needs of the Historical Sciences'; Dyer on 'The Needs of Biology'; and Nettleship on 'The Present Relations between Classical Research and Classical Education in England'.

[1] Cf. *The Times* (28 June 1876); M. Creighton, 'The Endowment of Research', *Macmillan's Magazine*, XXXIV (1876), 186–92; E. R. Lankester, 'The Endowment of Research', *Nature*, XIV (8 June 1876), 126–9; 'Essays on the Endowment of Research', *Dublin Review*, LXXXVIII (1876), 122. See also [W. Crookes], 'The Encouragement of Scientific Research', *Q.J. Sci.* VI (ns) (1876), 467–94.

[2] *The Spectator*, XLIX (10 July 1876), 899–900.

[3] *The World*, cited in *The Academy* (7 October 1876), 10.

[4] Appleton, *et al.* p. 235.

foreign scientific competition. With the Devonshire Reports, the claims for endowment of science by the State and by the universities were clearly before the public. The Oxford and Cambridge Act of 1877, passed after much debate, continued the direction taken since 1854. It gave the two universities a clearer footing *vis-à-vis* the colleges, and set up a new body of Executive Commissioners with powers to remodel the University and College Statutes. At best, however, the Commissioners could only use funds they could detach from the colleges for the Endowment of Research. Moreover, much to *Nature's* annoyance, the Commissioners included no one from outside the university circle.[1] The 'permissive' nature of the Act meant that progress depended upon co-operation between the colleges and the universities. By and large, most colleges, with a few exceptions, remained uncommitted to research. At Oxford, 'university' money was absorbed by new buildings, and little could be spared for stipends. A very few colleges (including Trinity, Balliol and Magdalen) maintained their own laboratories.[2]

The Executive Commissioners were still sitting in 1880 when Gladstone returned to power. Then, just as victory seemed within their reach, the reformers began to lose ground.

V. ENDOWMENT OF RESEARCH: OBSTACLES AND REACTIONS

It would be wrong to assume that the arguments of either the London reformers or the Oxford 'researchers' were ever accepted without question. Indeed, the delicate and intricate nature of research and the suitability of positive endowment raised questions of fundamental importance to the place of fundamental science in an open society. Broadly speaking, resistance to research developed in four areas; first, the issue was caught in the flotsam of delayed political promises. The *Essays* and the final Devonshire Report coincided with the great wave of reforming legislation in trade union policy, housing, public health and food and drugs regulation that fell

---

[1] [William Jack] (Professor at Manchester), 'The Universities Bill', *Nature*, xvi (3 May 1877), 1–2.
[2] Sir Harold Hartley, 'The Contribution of the College Laboratories', *Chemistry in Oxford* (London, 1966), pp. 7–10.

to the lot of Disraeli's first administration. University reform was a relatively easy matter in some ways, as it cost little public money, and won political favour in certain quarters. But the Government could argue, with some justice, that its hands were too full to take on the larger task of reorganising science, particularly as there was no strong political mandate to do so, and because scientists themselves were not united on what should be done. In any case, to implement all the Devonshire recommendations would have cost a great deal over a long period of time. And in terms of political realities, little favour could be won from the electorate by the Conservatives for reforms of institutions which still affected an exceedingly small section of society, many of whom had Liberal politics. Richard Proctor warned against taxing people for science. In particular, a new ministry, as Strange had recommended:

having, as an important part of its duty, the control of large sums of money for researchers of only philanthropic interest, would certainly be objected to by the country at large, and ... might excite a hostility to science and to scientific men which would most seriously injure the prospects of science in this country.[1]

In place of general approval of the Commission's recommendations, came frequent criticism of bias among its witnesses, and expressions of caution and restraint towards any wide scheme of endowment that would bring about 'scientific Micawberism'.[2] Some specific recommendations, particularly the relatively inexpensive ones, were accepted. Disraeli's administration established a museum collection of scientific apparatus and over opposition from the Royal Astronomical Society virtually endowed Lockyer with a solar physics observatory. The science schools at South Kensington were consolidated from the fragmentary bits of educational apparatus under the wing of the Science and Art Department, and the parliamentary grant for scientific research was increased from £1,000 to £5,000 p.a.

In any event the Conservatives remained in office for too short a time to implement a long-term programme, even if such a programme had been feasible. When Gladstone returned

[1] R. Proctor, 'Money for Science', *Cornhill Magazine*, xxxii (1875), 463.
[2] *Ibid.* p. 470.

to power in 1880 and again in 1886 and 1892, the Liberal 'reformers', with their chronic emphasis on retrenchment, brought the 'researchers' grave disappointment. Gladstone, never a friend of science at the best of times, set himself against the notion of a centralised Ministry of Science on constitutional grounds, and against State intervention in science on the principle of 'free trade and no favour'.

Not surprisingly, men of science lost faith in both parties. The Conservatives, said one reviewer, gave forth hostile cries of 'confiscation, spoilation, violation, communism, revolution, pious founders and the like', and announced to the reformers: 'If you want places for the advance and increase of human knowledge, found them and endow them yourselves.' The same writer found Liberalism standing 'mute, fearing lest its Chinese idol, competitive examination, should be overthrown and his joss house burnt in the struggle'.[1]

Perhaps even more critical to research than the realities of party politics were the successive tides of intellectual opposition to science and scientific methods that swept through the 1870s and 1880s. Science had gradually severed its connections with theology, and the separation had become widely accepted. Gladstone in 1881 ruled decisively that the debate had come to an impasse; 'let the scientific men stick to their science and leave philosophy and religion to poets, philosophers and theologians'. Looking back in 1879 over two decades of public resistance to Darwinism, W. K. Clifford optimistically reflected that 'such distrust or dislike of science ... as is to be found among us is due to circumstances which are rapidly disappearing, to misunderstanding and imperfect training ... a tendency in the expounders of scientific doctrine to make too sure of things, to put forward as known fact that which is not yet known fact, but only conjecture'.[2] But Clifford's optimism was premature. By the early 1880s science had cut itself off from much popular sympathy and support. Individualists saw in science no longer a wand of limitless progress, but a sword of intellectual and moral subjugation. Amid increasing specialisation, the British Association was

---

[1] [W. Crookes], 'The Encouragement of Scientific Research', *Q.J. Sci.* VI (ns) (1876), 486.
[2] W. K. Clifford, *Lectures and Essays* (London, 1870), p. 243.

losing its generalist character.[1] Under attack by social reformers like Frances Power Cobbe, men of science were accused of 'scientific arrogance', and of attempting to supplant traditional loyalties by a 'priestcraft of science', possessing attitudes less and less comprehensible to the average man.[2] As Clerk Maxwell confessed, all scientists were 'supposed to be in league with the material spirit of the age' forming 'a kind of advanced Radical party among men of learning'.[3]

For wide sections of the public, the concepts of Unity and Uniformity in Nature, wrought first by geology, then by cell theory and the laws of thermodynamics, brought the threatening prospect of an encompassing, atheistic materialism. This not only made scientists suspect, but brought the pursuit of science – an activity proclaimed as benevolent, useful and moral by Lord Brougham and the Society for the Diffusion of Useful Knowledge fifty years before[4] – into grave disrepute. Nothing brought this change in attitudes quite so clearly home as the reaction to John Tyndall's Belfast Address in 1874.[5]

Throughout the 1880s, certain literary reviewers repeatedly

[1] O. J. R. Howarth, *The British Association for the Advancement of Science: A Retrospect, 1831–1931* (London, 1931).

[2] Frances Power Cabbe, *The Scientific Spirit of the Age* (London, 1888).

[3] Clerk Maxwell, *Introductory Lecture on Experimental Physics* (London 1871), p. 17.

[4] See e.g. J. W. Hays, 'Science and Brougham's Society', *Annals of Science*, xx (1964), 227–41.

[5] The intellectual crisis of the 1870s is well illustrated in the history of the Metaphysical Society, which began in 1869 in an attempt to 'unite all shades of religious opinion against materialism'. See Alan Brown, *The Metaphysical Society, Victorian Minds in Crisis, 1869–1880* (New York, 1947), pp. 21 *et passim.* The impact of reductionism, atomism, scientific materialism was darkly illuminated by Tennyson, first in his poem *Lucretius* and later, more optimistically, in the *Higher Pantheism.* For reactions to Tyndall, who more than once had 'severely tried the patience not merely of the public but of a large number of his scientific brethren by the rashness with which he had intruded his speculations into regions far beyond those who are properly the province of the Professor of Natural Science', see [Henry Wace], 'Scientific Lectures – their Use and Abuse', *Quarterly Review*, cxiv (1878), 35–61, esp. 38–9. See also A. S. Eve and C. H. Creasy, *The Life of John Tyndall* (London, 1945), ch. xv. The Belfast Address was published separately by Longmans, with an explanation by Tyndall in September 1874, and was reprinted with modifications in Tyndall's *Fragments of Science* (London, 1894), 6th ed. vol. ii, p. 193. For an intermediate position on the 'errors of modern physics', see Tyndall's old enemy, Prof. P. G. Tait, *Lectures on some Recent Advances in Physical Science* (London, 1876), pp. 1–26.

denounced the 'arrogance' of scientists who identified man with the 'Kingdom of Nature', and by so doing reduced his laws and institutions – indeed the inductionist domain of rational free will – to the status of mere animal organisation, amenable to the studies of reductionist anthropology and psychology.[1] Social and intellectual resistance to physico-chemical reductionism was shortly followed and illustrated by larger, less specific and less intellectualised references to the 'degrading' tendencies of science, particularly those associated with research in Germany and France. The Reports of the Royal Commission on Vivisection in 1876 – shortly following the Devonshire Commission, and virtually coinciding with the *Essays* – inescapably connected the advancement of biological and physiological research with the iniquities of animal experimentation.[2]

If biology bred brutality, physics and chemistry brought materialism, and all 'pure' research, by implication, was suspect. One writer in the *Journal of Science* even argued that 'the life that is wholly given over to such pursuits (i.e. research) is a misspent one, and is, as an example, positively injurious to Society.'[3] An American critic speculated bitterly:

It is significant of the political immorality and readiness to tyrannise over others in the pursuit of their aims, which characterise the scientific classes, that they are willing to admire and support any government which is willing in return to endow their scholarships and erect their laboratories. They are inclined to surrender all political liberty, if by doing so they can obtain a ruler who will build them a number of new colleges, with every new instrument ready to their hands for animal torture and physiological or chemical experiment.[4]

---

[1] Robert Ward, 'Scientific Arrogance', *Q. J. Sci.* (3rd series), III (1881), 249–58.

[2] Cf. *Report of the Royal Commission on Vivisection* (1876), XL, p. 277. The ethics of vivisection were debated vigorously in the scientific press and the quarterlies. See *Nature*, XIV (25 May 1876); Stephen Coleridge, 'The Administration of the Cruelty to Animals Act of 1876', *Fortnightly Review*, LXVII (1900), 392–8. Vivisection was also the subject of a second Royal Commission which sat for five years, 1907–12 and issued four voluminous Reports. Not until 1912 could the Commission report public acceptance of the 'experimental method', and even then inserted a strong reservation against 'an exaggerated over-estimation of the usefulness of results obtained from experiments on animals'. *Final Report of the Royal Commission on Vivisection*, 1912 [Cd. 6114], xlviii, paras. 73–4 and pp. 129–31.

[3] Cited in Frank Fernseed, 'The Future Martyrdom of Science', *Q.J. Sci.* (3rd series), III (1881), 202.

[4] 'Some Fallacies of Science', *North American Review*, CXLII (1886), 151.

John Ruskin, speaking of Darwin and Tyndall, claimed that science should not be pursued as an end in itself, but should be subordinate to ethics. Where science clashed with ethics, science should give way. Thus, Ruskin opposed the new physical laboratory, built at Oxford in 1884.[1] His sentiments were often repeated out of context in the growing reaction against vivisection, vaccination and rabies inoculation in the 1880s and 1890s. National 'leagues' against vaccination and the notification of infectious diseases received wide popular support, particularly among the working classes in the north and London, but also among well-to-do middle-classes in the west of England. They were symptomatic of a broad wave of popular disillusionment with the implications of science.[2]

Within science there was also division and dissatisfaction. Many held that British science, noisily accompanied by public begging, was in danger of losing its 'dignity'.[3] The great principles of early nineteenth-century science which led to unity and convergence in scientific ideas had been advanced fairly cheaply in economic terms, and certainly without much state patronage. This ostensibly spoke volumes for the British national character, unfettered by financial strings of government gold. 'Hitherto, indeed', wrote Grant Allen, a well known populariser, in 1887, 'we Britons have been remarkable as the propounders of the deepest and widest scientific generalisations; it is only of late years that our bookish educators of the new school have conceived the noble ambition of turning us all into imitation Germans.'[4] 'Self-Help in Science' was still the most desirable state. But each new report from Germany

1 W. G. Collingwood, *John Ruskin: His Life and Work* (London, 1874), vol. II, pp. 90, 223.

2 R. MacLeod, 'Law, Medicine and Public Opinion: The Reaction to Compulsory Health Legislation, 1870–1907', *Public Law* (1967), 107–28, 189–211. Compare the vast protest literature connected with such women as Catherine Walter ('The Tyranny of Science', *New Science Review*, II (1895), 341–2) and Frances Power Cobbe, ('The Scientific Spirit of the Age', *Contemporary Review* LIV (1880), 126–39). See also [Anon], *Science in Excelsis* (London, 1875), with its parody of the 'Celestial Association for the Promotion of Science'. For analogous commentary in America see Noah Porter (then President of Yale), *Science and Sentiment* (May 1882).

3 Cf. R. Proctor, 'The Dignity of Science', *Knowledge* (1 January 1886), 93–5.

4 Grant Allen, 'The Progress of Science from 1836–1886', *Fortnightly Review*, XLI (1887), 873.

brought news that the 'bookish educators' seemed to be ushering in important research in electricity, in organic chemistry, in the chemical and physical foundations of astronomy, and developing increasingly expensive research in cellular biology and physiology. There were few ways of assessing or comparing the quality of British and German science, and it was all too easy to confuse the visible power of technological achievement with the less visible 'potential' of pure science. But the level of organisation set by German example had much to recommend it, and romantic analogies with starving poets drawn by Samuel Smiles and Grant Allen found few supporters within science itself.

There were also strong feelings within science that science should not become the servant of Government. An 'FRS' deplored in a letter to *The Times* in September 1876 the current 'wretched whining cry for State funds in aid of research'.

Hitherto there has generally existed among scientific men in this country a healthy spirit of independence, and it is earnestly to be hoped that it may long continue, and not be found to bow the knee to some official Baal and 'walk after things that do not profit'.[1]

There were also men of science who saw the entire Devonshire Commission as the 'mere tools and catspaws of a needy and designing confederacy' led by Strange and Lockyer.[2] It was charged that Lockyer, having a large family, persuaded the Government to give him a 'berth' merely for personal reasons. This could not be proved.[3] But the innuendo caused resentment among government astronomers in particular, and within the metropolitan scientific community in general.

In 1876, Richard Proctor published a book entitled *Wages and Wants of Science Workers*, in which he argued that the resources of science should be privately won. 'Pure science does not need to go begging for State subsidies', he claimed.[4]

---

[1] *The Times* (16 September 1876).
[2] *English Mechanic* (7 January 1876), 415.　　　　　　　　　[3] *Ibid.*
[4] Richard B. Proctor, *Wages and Wants of Science Workers* (London, 1876). Cf. an enthusiastic review in *The English Mechanic* (7 January 1876), 415: 'Of all the contributions to the literature of the *vexato questo* of the endowment of scientific research which have hitherto appeared, there is scarcely one which seems to us so well calculated to diffuse sound and just views on the subject and to enlighten the general public as to the real end and aim of those who clamour for it.'

If men of science descended into official or salaried posts they would lose their disinterestedness. A profusion of official posts and subsidies would not only deprive popular literature of its best and most regular contributors – men who had 'ennobled themselves by being forced to live by their pens' – but would also create a sense of cross materialism within science. The State would produce 'scientific Micawberism'.[1] Proctor felt that more government money should be spent on utilitarian science, but that support for pure research should come from the universities themselves.

This view did not commend itself to the 'researchers', although the Oxford group, by now a silent minority, would not have opposed it. Indeed, the Oxford movement had nearly died with Appleton's death in 1879. The whole weight of the 'research movement' outside the universities fell upon Lockyer and his associates. Although reforms were gradually occurring in the universities, these received less public attention. Some university reformers found the movement's deflection a timely relief. But it meant that attention was now concentrated, perhaps more than circumstances warranted, on those who were researchers rather than teachers, and who placed a higher value on science than on university reform in science. One such enterprise was the 'Birmingham Research Fund', begun in 1880 by the Birmingham Philosophical Society (itself founded only in 1876). The first decision of the fund was to award George Gore £150 for three years. *Nature* reported the news with thanksgiving: 'Perhaps nothing would sooner convince our ignorant and one-sided politicians of the reality of science and of the necessity for its national recognition, than [similar] efforts ... in all our great industrial centres.'

Beginning in 1880–1, Lockyer and his associates became embroiled in a lengthy debate, particularly visible in the *English Mechanic*, a heady rival of *Nature* which boasted a circulation larger than all other English scientific publications put together.[2] 'FRAS', a regular correspondent in the *English Mechanic*, claimed that those 'who were the most pushing and clamorous before the Royal Commission were those *who wanted the money themselves* (sic)'. They were not really among the 'best' scientists anyway, FRAS archly claimed: 'It is the

---

[1] Proctor, p. 86.   [2] *English Mechanic*, XII (23 September 1870), Editorial.

pseudo-scientific men, the quacks, advertisers and begging letters of the scientific world who are clamouring to be subsidised.' Indeed, he argued, taking a broad swing at Lockyer and the South Kensington Science School:

> The 'Endowment of Research' has come in these later days to signify the subsidising of such things as 'Committees on Solar Physics', and not in the very slightest degree the helping of the real student. It means the opening of the National Purse, the shutting of the Nation's eyes, and the seeing what Brompton will send us.[1]

Through 1881, allegations mounted against the 'endowment intrigue', and against the 'Brompton pluralists', each of whom held central posts already.[2] The *English Mechanic* claimed that *The Times*, the *Daily News*, the *Academy* and *Nature* were sealed to its protests,[3] and was probably quite right, given the pervasive influence of Lockyer and the X-Club. Indeed, its recriminations had some following in 'respectable' circles.

Without descending to personal comment, resistance against the 'researchers' arose among certain scientists in government service, who preferred to have government expenditure confined to government departments. Some of these contributed support to a Society for Opposing the Endowment of Research, of which Captain W. Noble, the astronomer, was Honorary Secretary. In February 1881, Sir George Airy, Astronomer Royal, advanced the conservative position of this group, in a letter to Captain Noble, published in the *English Mechanic*.

> I think [he said] that successful researches have in nearly every instance originated with private persons, or with persons whose positions were so nearly private ... that the investigators acted under private influence, without the dangers attending connection with the State.
>
> Certainly I do not consider a Government as justified in endeavouring to force at public expense investigations of undefined character, and at best of doubtful utility; and I think it probable that any such attempts will lead to consequences disreputable to science.[4]

In 1882, the question was debated again at the Social Science Association. The case as put by Rowland Hamilton, Secretary of the Education Section, was simple: 'Endowment' meant that 'those who were engaged in research should, upon due proof that they were engaged, be exempt from carking cares

---

[1] *English Mechanic* (17 December 1880), 349.   [2] *Ibid.* (11 February 1881), 539.
[3] *Ibid.* (6 May 1881), 208.   [4] *Ibid.* (25 February 1881), 586–7.

and difficulties'. There was no doubt that 'at present any object of research must be investigated by people of independent means'. Such means should exist for men of quality without making them feel 'under a personal obligation to anyone'.[1]

From this and other discussions, however, it was clear that those 'researchers' outside the universities had not worked out *who* would administer government grants, to whom they would be given, and what criteria would be used. Without precise arrangements of this kind, proposals for large scale research schemes inevitably fanned controversy. Even existing research schemes had not proved wholly satisfactory. Indeed, there were those, like Airy, who contended with some justification that 'the world ... is not unanimous in believing that [the Royal Society's Government Grant] have been useful. It is commonly acknowledged, even by supporters of research, that they were awarded in a "lax and unbusinesslike way".'[2] In a sense, the early difficulties of the GFC had, by 1881, played into the hands of those who opposed the endowment of research.

It was true that the position advocating 'payments by results' was far easier for the Treasury to accept. But even where science proceeded by 'results' in government scientific establishments, there could be disadvantages. Sir William Flower, director of the Natural History Museum, admitted in 1898 that when 'curatorships of this or that division of science are founded and endowed, their holders are usually tenacious either of encroachment upon or wide enlargement of the boundaries of the subject they have undertaken to teach or illustrate; and in this way, more than any other, passing phases of scientific knowledge have been crystallised or fossilised in institutions where [this] might least have been expected'.[3] The risks of narrowness seemed to many preferable to the risk of supporting undefined research. But who was finally to judge the merits of either approach?

Given such wide social and professional differences within science the Treasury naturally looked to the Royal Society for guidance. For reasons both administrative and traditional,

---

[1] *Knowledge*, II (29 September 1882), 296; *Transactions of the Social Science Association* (Nottingham, 1883), 319–30.
[2] *English Mechanic* (22 July 1881), 472.
[3] Sir W. H. Flower, *Essays on Museums and Other Subjects Connected with Natural History* (London, 1898), p. 11.

the Royal Society was unwilling to become wholly responsible for awarding full-cost payments for original research. Since the 1870s, the Society itself had come under increasing public scrutiny. Public interest in science had fostered growing concern about the Society's activity, and there were those who deprecated change. In December 1880, *The Times* remarked disparagingly that 'the election to the vacancies in its ranks has of late years been too manifestly governed by a tendency to set up as an idol something which it is technically fashionable to call "research" and to ignore the far higher mental effort which is required for successful ratiocination'.[1] Given this pressure, Hooker's policies of 1876 were kept alive for nearly a generation. The Royal Society stood aloof, and continued to foster the ideal of science for its own sake without assuming responsibility for the individual consequences of this activity.[2]

Under the circumstances, the Treasury had either to continue to limit its support of science to the provision of apparatus and publications, as it had always done, or else be persuaded of the 'utility' of supporting free and unfettered research. It was not immediately obvious that it would be useful to pay someone without having a clear idea of what he would do, or what would come from the expenditure. In 1881, A. J. Mundella, then Vice-President of the Council, acted on the recommendations of the GFC and tried to increase the value of personal grants to £3,000 per year. Moreover, he proposed to endow, under the Science and Art Department, an enlarged programme of 18 to 20 'State Fellowships' for science, costing £200 to £400 apiece, amounting to £2,000 p.a. But the Treasury rejected Mundella's plans: 'I think it most mischievous to make a Parliamentary Department the channel of doles,' Ralph Lingen (Permanent Secretary) observed.[3] Such an act would 'bring the State into a relation with individual scientific investigation which it is most undesirable that it should occupy'.[4] It would also doubtless

[1] *The Times* (2 December 1880).
[2] Some of these consequences I have dealt with elsewhere. See R. MacLeod, 'Scientists, Civil Servants and the Support of Fundamental Research: The Government Grant Fund of the Royal Society, 1850–1914', *Hist. J.* xiv, 2 (1971), 323–58.
[3] T1/8008C/20599, Minute, *c.* 3 February 1882.
[4] T1/8008C/20599, Lingen to Cavendish, 2 February 1882.

have brought the Treasury little pleasure. Lingen was willing
enough to let the Royal Society, as the respected representative
of British Science, have its grant. But 'Fellowships' awarded
directly by Government could not meet his high Gladstonian
standards of accountability. Thus:

A small grant [like the Royal Society equipment grant] ... has many
advantages. The real workers whose work is known to be worth much are
few and a small grant obliges selection. It also escapes question. A large
grant soon attracts the Parliamentary Philistine (asking) 'well – what have
you got for your money?' – the question is legitimate and fatal. That is
why I think the state is better away.[1]

In a compromise with the Treasury, Mundella's plan was
exchanged for an arrangement whereby the Royal Society's
funds were reduced by £1,000 but which gave the Society
greater freedom to manage its remaining grant. From 1882 to
1900 the government grant remained at £4,000. But the
principle of personal stipends had been conceded. By the mid
1880s the resistance to research had begun to ebb. One of
the last volleys of opposition was fired by Richard Proctor
in his own journal, *Knowledge*, shortly before his death in
1884. 'Few circumstances have caused true lovers of science
in recent times more pain than that outcry for the Endowment of Research', he wrote, in an essay which ended with a
personal sally against Lockyer. The volley was ignored. By
and large, the 'researchers' had won.

VI. CONFLUENCE AND CONSOLIDATION 1890–1900

The endowment of science movement of the 1860s and 1870s,
followed by the counter-movement of the 1880s, was followed
in turn by a gradual acceptance of the principle of endowment.
Institutes for fundamental research, supported both by
governmental and private benefactions, gradually emerged.
The London School of Tropical Medicine, which concentrated
on research, was established in 1899 by the Colonial Office
under Joseph Chamberlain. An Imperial Research Fund was
launched in 1901 for the study of cancer. Private endowments
for bacteriological research were begun at the Jenner (now the
Lister) Institute, and the Davy–Faraday Laboratory for

[1] T1/8008C/20599, Lingen to Cavendish, 2 February 1881.

physical chemistry at the Royal Institution was opened with a gift from Alfred Mond.[1] The *Daily Telegraph* greeted the Mond bequest with a calm acceptance of the obvious. 'Nothing', it observed, 'is better worth buying than scientific fact.' With pardonable licence the *Telegraph* speculated that the Mond grant could possibly do 'more for physical science at one stroke than all the Cabinets of Her Majesty have done since the commencement of that reign, one of the greatest glories of which has been the advance of research in England'.[2]

But neither these institutes nor government departments could meet the needs of 'researchers' for salaries and fellowships. The government grant scheme lagged behind the growing number of young men of science, while the Treasury looked cynically at the alleged 'nest-building' of Lockyer and the Science and Art Department at South Kensington.[3] As the Royal Society remained dispassionate and uninvolved, it remained for the universities to provide the base on which 'researchers' could build on a significant scale. In 1850 there were about sixty university posts in science and technology (excluding medicine, but including agriculture) in Britain; by 1900, there were over 400. Government assistance, when it came to the universities from 1889 onwards, came principally by way of subsidies in aid of teaching, but this inevitably acted as an indirect endowment of research. The development of 'research schools' in the late 1890s, notably at the Cavendish, set the pattern. In 1894, largely through the efforts of Lockyer, Mundella, Huxley and Playfair, money from the Royal Commission for the Exhibition of 1851 was used to begin the first imperial fellowship scheme for scientific research. One of the first '1851 Exhibitioners' was Ernest Rutherford.[4] The numbers of research fellowships tenable at universities and university colleges also increased. By 1914 there were 170 privately endowed fellowships for science at 24 different

---

[1] Cf. *The Times*, 'A Magnificent Endowment' (3 July 1894); *The Academy* (7 July 1894).
[2] *Daily Telegraph* (4 July 1894).
[3] *The Times* (23 December 1896).
[4] A. Gray, 'Fellowships for Research', *Nature*, LVIII (20 October 1898); R. MacLeod and E. Kay Andrews, 'Education, Career and Migration Patterns among Commission of 1851 Scholars: A Case Study in the Endowment of Research', *Nature*, CCXVIII (1968), 1011–16.

institutions (outside Oxford and Cambridge). These had the long-term effect of giving research a firm academic foundation, protected by traditions of freedom in learning and teaching and not subject to Treasury control or party politics.

Opponents of endowment still argued that by spending time in research 'the prospects of such men would be so injured that it would be difficult for them after to find congenial employment'. Well into the new century, a scientific man's 'prospects' remained very limited. But by 1914 *Who's Who in Science* listed over 1,600 leading men of science in Britain who had in some way found 'congenial employments'. In any event, the research community was increasing. In the 42 years between 1858 and 1900 the main research degree in science in England – the London D.Sc. – had only 171 successful candidates, while in the 14 years between 1900 and 1914, 108 more received the degrees. The static assumptions of the Treasury, which had limited the government grant to £4,000 per year while the number of British research workers doubled, and doubled again, had proved baseless. Moreover, as public opinion became persuaded of the needs of fundamental inquiry, the Gladstonian system of 'payment by results' could no longer be invoked as a magic phrase to reject all claims for 'unfettered research'.

There still remained great difficulties which the scientific reform movement had only partially resolved. Most British universities gave greater emphasis to education than to research training and 'research schools' were not visible in many universities until after the First World War. Moreover, despite the improved 'prospects of science', industry took little interest in research and there were few posts to absorb the growing numbers of research workers. It followed from this industrial indifference that research workers as a class, distinct from the chemists and physicists who led the professional institutions of the 1870s and 1880s, had less and less to do with applied science. Some posts were created at the National Physical Laboratory, which in many ways acted as a 'half-way house' between industry and the universities, but it became a commonplace article of British belief 'that there is one Science' and the University was its teacher.[1]

[1] *Nature*, CIV (6 November 1919), 257.

Resources of science in Victorian England

By 1900 it was often observed that Britain was falling behind Germany and even further behind America in numbers of science graduates and was employing her graduates outside industrial research. In 1900, there were about 2,000 men of science of graduate standing in Britain, about half of whom were secondary and primary schoolteachers; about 420 (18 per cent) were university teachers, and about 250 (10 per cent) were in the civil service. There were only about 225–50 graduate chemists in British industry. Between 1900 and 1914 the momentum generated by the 'researchers'' campaign began finally to show results. In these years alone the supply of science graduates reached nearly 6,000, of whom 300 received advanced degrees. By 1914 there were probably well over 7,000 graduate scientists in Britain and more with advanced degrees than there had been scientists altogether in 1850.[1]

Unwittingly, the endowment of research movement had helped drive a barrier between science and its industrial applications. By the 1890s the competition for university posts tended to select for early brilliance and grant high social rewards for pure research. Since fellowships were 'prizes' and went to the 'best', it was easily concluded that those who did not get them, and who therefore went into industry or teaching, were therefore not the 'best'. Provincial universities copied the fellowship pattern previously followed in Oxford, Cambridge and London. The 'best' – 'the generals of science' – won their prizes, while the 'second-' and 'third-' class minds, which Huxley called the 'rank and file' of science and which was visibly one major source of Germany's technological power, received little benefit from the endowment of research movement, from the Royal Society, or from the universities. Beginning in 1905, under Lockyer's leadership, the British Science Guild tried to draw public attention to the need for more scientists to be better deployed. But despite Lockyer's enthusiasm and the support of Lord Haldane, the British Science Guild failed to win significant industrial or governmental support. Indeed, provision for industrial research was not increased significantly until national demands precipitated

[1] R. M. Pike, *The Growth of Scientific Institutions and Employment of Natural Science Graduates in Britain, 1900–1960* (Unpublished MSc dissertation, University of London, 1961).

by the war placed the importance of relating fundamental to industrial research firmly among the leading priorities of the state.

VII. CONCLUSION

The endowment of research movement can be seen in five distinct phases. The first, 1850–1869 saw successive stages of investigation and reform in the universities, the emergence of the London circle, and the manoeuvres of the British Association which culminated in the Devonshire Commission. This phase was followed between 1870 and 1875 by the growth of a working alliance between Oxford-based university reformers and the London circle – men of widely differing social class and scholarly attitude – who proclaimed in *Nature* and the *Academy* their recommendations for endowment and reform. Between 1876 and 1880 this alliance developed into the endowment of science movement proper, which reached a climax in the eighth report of the Devonshire Commission, the publication of Appleton's *Essays*, the extension of the Government Grant Fund, and the enactment of the university reform Acts. The same period, however, also witnessed growing opposition to research on social, ethical and economic grounds. This resistance became stronger in the fourth phase between 1880 and 1885, reflected in growing hostility towards Lockyer, the collapse of the Oxford reformist wing, and the distraction of government by more pressing issues of domestic and imperial policy. Victory for the 'researchers', however, drew near in the fifth phase from 1885 to 1900 when university, government and private research establishments and fellowship schemes were begun. Between 1900 and 1915, the efforts of the 'researchers' were finally vindicated in the creation of state fellowships for research, including those of the Development Commission and the Department of Scientific and Industrial Research.

In many respects, the endowment of research movement broke new ground. Unlike the 'Decline of Science' debate half a century before, the 'researchers' movement' witnessed few calls for public honours or recognition. Instead, it sought a fundamental change in the way in which the Government and universities viewed science. Research claimed to be a national resource, like labour and capital, a productive factor to be cultivated. A new principle was to be invoked. Labourers would be paid not by results, but according to promise, with the anticipation of useful contributions if they were left to follow their own bent. This principle incorporated in the concept of the 'research fellowship' represented a great act of faith on the part of the reformers, before which the Treasury not unreasonably paused.

To assure Government and the public that science would bring practical and beneficial results, to overcome Treasury scruples, and to negotiate carefully a programme of progress through waves of social disenchantment with the assumptions and image of science, were formidable tasks. The endowment of research movement left an important inheritance. One part of that inheritance was a sense of association, by which a body of scientists, divided perhaps in social attitudes and personal philosophy, could be bound together by shared convictions and could plead those convictions through press, public meetings and deputations. In this sense the endowment of research movement helped to create the impression that scientists could be identified by certain unifying attitudes and could be considered a collective 'community' within society.

In the political atmosphere of the 1870s and 1880s – indeed until Balfour and Haldane lifted research out of neglect in the 1890s and 1900s – there was little possibility of achieving in England a sense of political urgency in the support of science. The history of the movement showed that research had not only to justify itself, but had to be seen to justify itself. Specialised research was in many fields elaborating, consolidating, and framing new questions for science, but only a fraction of this activity could be seen to result in ameliorative technology. In the absence of such justification, scientific research would be given a low priority by a political system preoccupied with immediate problems of imperial expansion, economic unrest, inadequate housing, unsystematic education, poverty and unemployment. In a sense, the 'researchers'' victory was a paradox. The public acceptance that brought them recognition in universities and research institutes also helped separate them from industry and society at large. The implications of this separation were profound. By its very success the endowment of research movement had helped to sow fundamental questions about the social function of science in modern society.